THUS SAITH THE LORD?

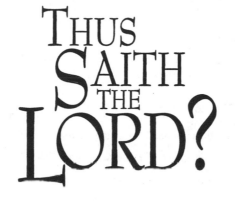

John Bevere

THUS SAITH THE LORD? by John Bevere
Published by Creation House
Strang Communications Company
600 Rinehart Road
Lake Mary, Florida 32746
Web site: http://www.creationhouse.com

Unless otherwise noted, Scripture quotations are from the New King James Version of the Bible. Copyright © 1979, 1980, 1982 by Thomas Nelson, Inc., publishers. Used by permission.

Scripture quotations marked AMP are from the Amplified Bible. Old Testament copyright © 1965, 1987 by the Zondervan Corporation. The Amplified New Testament copyright © 1954, 1958, 1987 by the Lockman Foundation. Used by permission.

Scripture quotations marked KJV are from the King James Version of the Bible.

Scripture quotations marked NAS are from the New American Standard Bible. Copyright © 1960, 1962, 1963, 1968, 1971, 1972, 1973, 1975, 1977 by the Lockman Foundation. Used by permission.

Scripture quotations marked NCV are from The Holy Bible, New Century Version. Copyright © 1987, 1988, 1991 by Word Publishing, Dallas, Texas 75039. Used by permission.

Scripture quotations marked NIV are from the Holy Bible, New International Version. Copyright © 1973, 1978, 1984, International Bible Society. Used by permission.

Scripture quotations marked NLT are from the Holy Bible, New Living Translation, copyright © 1996. Used by permission of Tyndale House Publishers, Inc., Wheaton, IL 60189. All rights reserved.

Scripture quotations marked CEV are from the Contemporary English Version, copyright © 1995 by the American Bible Society. Used by permission.

Interior design and layout by Lillian L. McAnally

Library of Congress Cataloging-in-Publication Data:
Bevere, John.
    Thus saith the Lord? / John Bevere.
    p. cm.
ISBN: 0-88419-575-9
1. Prophecy—Christianity.   I. Title
BR115.P8B48 1999   99-11625
234`.13—dc21   CIP

9012345 BBG 8765432
Printed in the United States of America

I dedicate this book to all those called to prophetic ministry. God says:

> If you extract the precious from the worthless, you will become My spokesman.
>
> —JEREMIAH 15:19, NAS

May His heart be revealed through you to His people.

Acknowledgments

My deepest appreciation to...

My wife, Lisa—next to the Lord, you are my dearest friend and greatest love. Thank you for the hours of editing you contributed to this book. I love you!

Our four sons, Addison, Austin, Alexander, and Arden—all of you have brought great joy to my life. You are each a special treasure to me. Thank you for sharing in the call of God and encouraging me to travel and write.

Loran Johnson—thank you for the love, kindness, and wisdom you have selflessly given to our family and ministry. You are a true friend and disciple of Jesus.

Pastor Al Brice—you have seen our weaknesses and walked with us through our shortcomings over our many years of friendship, yet you have loved Lisa and I all the more. Thanks for being a true brother and pastor.

The staff of John Bevere Ministries—thank you for your unwavering support and faithfulness. Lisa and I love each of you.

David and Pam Graham—thank you for your sincere and faithful support in overseeing the operations of our European office.

Rory and Wendy Alec—thanks for believing in the message God has placed in our hearts. We treasure your friendship.

Deborah and Barbara—thank you for your editing skills in this project. But most of all, thanks for your encouragement and support.

Most important, my sincere gratitude to my Lord. How can words adequately acknowledge all You have done for me and for Your people? I love You more than I will ever be able to express. I will love You forever!

Ahhhh! Finally a breath of fresh air on the often-confusing subject of prophecy. John Bevere has gotten down to the core of truth. Thus Saith the Lord? *is a gem of insight and honesty. With this book, Bevere has cleared the air and given us a key to the door of discernment.*

—TED HAGGARD
NEW LIFE CHURCH
COLORADO SPRINGS, CO

FOREWORD

One of the ministry gifts being restored by the Holy Spirit is the prophetic ministry. Just as the truth of healing has been restored to the church, or the baptism in the Holy Spirit with its related spiritual *charismata* has been restored, so has the fivefold ministry of apostle, evangelist, pastor, teacher, and prophet.

Yet it seems that when something good is restored to the church, excesses inevitably occur. And in the process, people are sometimes hurt—some so seriously that it causes them to become bitter or to fall into unbelief.

For example, if someone is desperate for healing, believes in healing, and yet is not healed, that person is often disillusioned and devastated. If someone submits to a pastor and is abused by that pastor in some way, he or she may leave the church disheartened, afraid to ever trust a pastor again.

The area of the restoring of the prophetic seems most apt to be misunderstood or abused. Many Christians don't accept prophetic gifts as necessary for today, believing that God does not still speak to His people through prophets. If they do get over that hurdle and believe prophecy is for today—even for *themselves* or *their families*—they may still fall prey to being disappointed or even deceived by those who prophesy to them. They may accept any "word" that comes from a "prophet" as being from the Lord Himself. Others, excited about words they receive, begin to follow those with prophetic gifts—sometimes more than Christ Himself.

In my role as publisher of *Charisma* magazine, I have observed the Holy Spirit's restoration of prophetic ministry in the church. God has raised up prophetic voices in our generation. My family and I have been blessed and encouraged by the prophecies we have received from some with prophetic ministries.

Recently in my own Bible study I've noticed Bible stories that seem similar to the personal prophetic ministry we see at times today. In Genesis 18 we read about three men who visit Abraham and tell him that by the same time next year Sarah will bear a son! Sarah laughed, believing she and Abraham were too old, but Isaac was born later that year.

Even the ministry of Jesus included His encounter with the woman at the well of Samaria, where He told her how many times she had been married and that the man with whom she was living was not her husband. In astonishment she replied to Jesus, "Sir, I perceive that You are a prophet" (John 4:19). Then she told her friends to "come, see a Man who told me all things that I ever did" (John 4:29).

While I have been personally blessed by prophetic ministry and believe it is a valid ministry to the church, I am increasingly alarmed by abuses that are occurring. *Charisma* did an in-depth report recently about a ministry that "sold" prophecies for donations of certain amounts. The bigger the donation, the more in-depth the prophecy. Another time a respected television ministry raised millions of dollars as one of their guests gave out "words" to donors who sent in donations for its telethon.

What can be done?

I believe God has placed certain people in the body of Christ to sound the alarm when something goes wrong. The late Jamie Buckingham, my long-time mentor, was such a man. When the Discipleship movement fell into error in the 1970s, he confronted the error by boldly proclaiming the truth in his pointed articles and in some of his books.

How much better for someone like Jamie, who loved the people involved, to confront the issue than to leave it to those critics who make a living attacking those of us who believe in the fullness of the Holy Spirit and in spiritual gifts. The witch hunts some critics have conducted have accomplished very little except to embarrass the church.

In the same way that the physical body has white corpuscles in the blood to ward off disease, the body of Christ needs men and women of conviction to point out where we stray from the pure gospel and to draw us back to the straight and narrow—back to Christ.

I believe John Bevere is such a man. In the past few years God has raised him up as a voice to remind the church of the danger of holding on to offenses and to call the church to a new understanding of the fear of the Lord.

Now John writes a bold new book, which he believes may be one of his most important to date. He sees the devastation that comes when those with prophetic giftings get into error. He recognizes the trap of giving pleasant prophecies just because there is a desire on the part of some Christians to hear them. He identifies the casual habit of giving "words" as "thus saith the Lord" when the words are actually just personal opinion—not the oracles of God.

John Bevere does not call himself a prophet, nor is he "known" in this role in the body of Christ. Yet I believe John *is* a prophet, often crying in the wilderness just as his namesake John the Baptist.

In this book John is sounding an alarm. He is pointing back to the Scriptures as the measure of what is sound and false prophecy. But he does it without calling names, and what he writes is written in love, unlike some critics who only criticize out of a harsh, hateful spirit in order to tear down rather than build up.

I believe that in the same way an evangelist can stray from his primary call to bring people to repentance, or that a pastor can *hurt* rather than *heal* his flock, a prophetic voice can sometimes create havoc in people's lives that wasn't meant to be.

I challenge those who have prophetic giftings—from nationally known ministries to local Christians whose giftings open ministry doors in their own local church—to read this book carefully. They need to analyze it to be reminded of what the Scripture says and to see if their own ministries line up exactly with the Word of God.

Pastor Ted Haggard of New Life Church in Colorado Springs, Colorado made some excellent points in a recent issue of *Ministries Today:*[1]

> I concluded that false prophecy is a misuse of the Lord's name—which is a violation of the third commandment—and that people's fragile egos need to take a little heat if they are proclaiming themselves to be God's spokespersons and are not! After all, the Bible commands us to test prophecy to see if it really is of God (1 John 4:1).

Then Ted lists three levels of prophecy:

1. *"Thus saith the Lord"*

This is the highest form of prophecy. This is given when a believer is claiming to speak for God Himself. This type of prophecy is either 100 percent right or 100 percent wrong. Using this type of prophecy means that there can be no other opinions or contrary thought. Because the Lord has spoken, the discussion is over.

2. *"It seemed good to the Holy Spirit, and to us" (Acts 15:28)*

This type of prophecy reflects a general consensus about the will of God. It may or may not be 100 percent accurate, but by saying this a group is saying that to the best of their ability they believe this is the will of God for a particular situation.

3. *"Does this mean anything to you?" or "What do you think about this?"*

When, as we pray for people, a word or thought comes to mind, we can inquire of them what God is doing in their lives. Sometimes the Lord leads us into prophetic intercession. This could also be called a *word of knowledge* or a *word of wisdom* (1 Cor. 12:8). This type of prophecy makes no claims of authority.

Ted wraps up his article with this insight:

When I understood these three types of prophecy, it cleared the way in my heart to be more supportive of the various prophetic functions within the body of Christ. Without His prophetic function as a vital ingredient in our churches, we function without one of His greatest gifts, a fact that unnecessarily weakens our churches.

To which I say *amen.*

For those of us who will probably never have a prophetic ministry, we must read carefully what the Word of God says about those with prophetic ministries. In the same way that we evangelical Christians would not tolerate the preaching of pagan or false religion in our churches, or would reject a liberal theology that doesn't line up with the Word, we must be equally vigilant that prophetic ministries line up with the Word.

I believe John Bevere has a word for the church. He articulates it powerfully and with passion. I have carefully read this manuscript in its entirety because I feel its message is so important and needs to be understood and heeded by both Christian leaders and laity alike.

—STEPHEN STRANG, PUBLISHER
CHARISMA
LAKE MARY, FLORIDA

CONTENTS

Foreword vii

1 The Need for Prophetic Ministry 1

2 Widespread Deception 9

3 The True Prophetic Ministry I .19

4 The True Prophetic Ministry II 29

5 Prophetic Pollution 41

6 Personal Prophecy 55

7 Speaking to the Idols of the Heart 67

8 Defiled by Prophetic Words 85

9 Taught My People Rebellion .97

10 The Operation of Jezebel 109

11 Self or God Appointed 117

12 The Sting of Jezebel 127

13 Knowing Prophets by Their Fruit 139

14 The Love of the Truth 157

15 Testing and Handling Personal Prophecy 167

Epilogue 179

Notes 183

We have been so afraid of despising prophecy that we have neglected judging it.

1

THE NEED FOR
PROPHETIC MINISTRY

The greatest privilege and deepest desire of every believer is to hear God's voice. It was the cry of the Old Testament patriarchs who walked the desert sands. It was the longing of each New Testament believer to hear again the voice of God. Inherent in each of us is the desire to hear and know the Lord's voice.

It is a precious honor to sit at His feet and learn of Him. It is a treasure to be guarded. We are to set apart time to read His Word and then listen quietly for His still, small voice. This communion is to be cultivated, for it is a garden of provision, protection, and refreshing. Not unlike a marriage, it holds moments of intimate joy, secret longings, and unspeakable love. It is a place to bare our souls. It is a special and delicate relationship, one to be nourished and protected.

The ways God speaks to His children are various and many. I believe that His first preference is to speak directly to us. This is the very reason He sent His Son, so that the veil that separated man from God might be rent. This book does not attempt to cover the numerous ways God may choose to speak. It is a subject far too vast to address in just one volume. This book focuses on one specific aspect: how to know when God is speaking to you through another. This discernment is an integral part of your personal relationship with God.

It is an awesome responsibility to act as a message bearer "from God." Peter admonishes us, "If anyone speaks, he should do it as one speaking the very words of God" (1 Pet. 4:11, NIV). Paul confirms this is no light matter with, "I was with you in weakness, in fear, and in much trembling" (1 Cor. 2:3–6). Though we are human, God will entrust us with His precious voice and use us to speak His words to another.

A prophet is a divine spokesperson. To speak prophetically is to speak by divine inspiration. It is the presentation of God's message for an individual, group, nation, or generation. It may bring direction, correction, warning, encouragement, or instruction, but one thing is certain: *It will always direct the recipients to the heart and ways of God.* A messenger from God is only as good as he is faithful to the One he represents. He does not represent himself or his opinions. He represents God's.

MY FIRST ENCOUNTER WITH PERSONAL PROPHECY

I have been greatly ministered to by personal prophetic words. I remember the first time God spoke to me in this manner. The year was 1980. I was studying mechanical engineering at Purdue University. I had been saved two years earlier and soon afterward felt a strong tug on my heart toward ministry. My parents were not receptive to this due to our Catholic background. I found myself torn emotionally as I wavered back and forth. I respected my parents, but could not ignore the growing call I felt.

I attended a large conference with six to seven thousand others in Indianapolis, Indiana. The well-known minister concluded a wonderful message, then said God had given him words for two individuals. The first was for a Baptist pastor.

The second was for me. He said, "There is a young man in here tonight, and you are sitting in the last couple of rows on the bottom floor [my location]. You vacillate back and forth as to whether or not you are called to the ministry. One day you know you're called; the next day you think, *Am I really called?* God says you are indeed called to the full-time ministry and that He is going to use you in a wonderful way."

As he spoke I knew beyond any doubt God was speaking directly to me. The strong witness of His peace and presence filled my heart as I listened. I felt as though each word became a part of me. I noticed a weight had lifted from my soul. The next morning I had such joy. I knew it was a settled issue. No longer would I be double-minded and tormented. I completed my engineering degree, and by the summer of 1983 I was in the ministry full time, serving my pastor. That word finalized the assurance of the call of God on my life.

FLESH VS. PROMISE

The Bible reveals that prophetic ministry will play a crucial role in preparing the church for the Lord's return. Peter quoted the prophet Joel, who said that sons and daughters, menservants and maidservants will prophesy (Acts 2:16–18; Joel 2:28–31). The enemy knows this as well. He longs to cripple or pervert the prophetic and diminish its effectiveness. He wants the church to remain fleshly, for then the precious is mixed with the vile.

It comes as no surprise that a biblical pattern exists that applies to much of the current prophetic ministry. More often than not the Ishmael precedes the Isaac. Flesh will try to bring forth what only the Spirit can. Allow me to explain. When he was seventy-five, Abraham received a promise from God that he would have a son. After eleven years of waiting he and his wife devised a plan of action. Hagar, his wife's slave girl, was given to Abraham, and a son named Ishmael was born.

God allowed this and must have thought, *If they think they can bring forth My promise through their flesh; I will wait until Abram's reproductive system is dead. Then I'll bring forth My Son of promise.* Why? Because He will not allow flesh to glory in His sight! Thirteen more years passed, and both of them were dead reproductively (Rom. 4:19). Then Sarah conceived and gave birth to Isaac. Paul wrote:

> The son of the slave-wife was born in a human attempt to bring about the fulfillment of God's promise. But the son of

3

the freeborn wife was born as God's own fulfillment of his promise.

—GALATIANS 4:23, NLT

God has promised to restore the prophetic in full power before Jesus returns (Acts 3:20–21). This expectation permeates the church. However, I have witnessed flesh's attempt to bring forth what God has promised.

There is the prophetic ministry of promise born of the will of the Father and there is the prophetic ministry born of flesh and the will of man. What is the difference? Though both are conceived through a genuine desire to fulfill God's plan and promise, the one birthed by flesh must be maintained by flesh while the one birthed by the Spirit will be sustained by the Spirit. Flesh reproduces flesh and therefore speaks directly to the desires of man. Spirit reproduces spirit and therefore speaks forth the desire of God. The purpose of this book is to help you discern between the voices. For though the words of flesh may be pleasant to our ears, they will lead us into defilement, destruction, or possibly death. Words of the Spirit, even if initially unpleasant, lead you to the heart of God.

TEST ALL PROPHECY

Personally I've received numerous "Thus saith the Lord's . . . " over my past twenty years as a Christian. Of these, only a handful have proven to be truly words from God. If I had heeded a lot of them, today I would be one confused individual and most likely detoured from the will of God. The New Testament exhorts us:

> Do not quench (suppress or subdue) the [Holy] Spirit; do not spurn the gifts and utterances of the prophets [do not depreciate prophetic revelations nor despise inspired instruction or exhortation or warning.] But test and prove all things [until you can recognize] what is good; [to that] hold fast.
> —1 THESSALONIANS 5:19–21, AMP

We need prophecy in the church and are strongly warned not to

4

despise it. To despise something is to condemn or hate it. We have been so afraid of despising prophecy that we have neglected judging it. It is important we learn to recognize or discern the true from the false. Examine again Paul's words in verse 21:

> But test and prove all things [until you can recognize] what is good; [to that] hold fast.

This is the objective of this book. We cannot accept the false as true because we are afraid of rejecting the true as false; we must learn to separate the good from bad. Nor is it right to be so overly cautious and critical that we reject the true. At present I believe we err in Spirit-filled circles to the loose acceptance of every word. We casually shrug off inaccurate or carnal words as, "Oh, well. They just missed that one," or, "They are just growing in their gift." But no one should take casually anything tagged with "thus saith the Lord."

Israel erred in this direction as well. It came to the place where God said through the prophet Micah:

> If a liar and deceiver comes and says, "I will prophesy for you plenty of wine and beer," he would be just the prophet for this people!
>
> —MICAH 2:11, NIV

The New Living Translation is even stronger. It reads, "That's just the kind of prophet you would like!" God was saying, "You will embrace as prophetic anything that satisfies your carnal desires and appetites."

Paul says that we are to test and prove all things until we learn to recognize what is from God. Since we've erred to leniency, you may feel this book leans the other way. If it does, it is with the hope of bringing proper, godly balance. We must shine the light of God's Word brightly while examining prophecy in context.

HOW THIS BOOK CAME FORTH

Originally I had not planned to write this book, but a sequel to *The Fear of the Lord*. I spent months compiling scriptures and information, and the publisher even advertised it. Over dinner with the publisher and some of his staff, I shared some of the insights you will find in this book. I noticed he was quiet and attentive as I spoke.

Afterward the publisher asked me, "John, could you write this as your next book?"

Surprised, I questioned, "You mean in place of our existing plans?"

He said, "Yes."

I said, "Let me pray about it."

I diligently sought God's will through prayer. I shared the book idea with close friends that I trust, and they strongly encouraged me to write on this topic as well. Deep in my heart I knew I was to do it, but I also knew it could upset some and be misunderstood by others. "Lord," I questioned, "do You really want me to write this book?" I could not help but think of the persecution it might bring. "Why should I bring persecution on myself?"

I found myself crying. I knew I was being selfish. I remembered the many people I have met and the stories I have heard of those who had been defiled by words that were not genuine. I decided I could not draw back from what God entrusted me to declare.

In this book I have included true stories that I believe will help you learn to identify the real from the false. No names are mentioned because this is not about identifying individuals, but about identifying error. With the exception of two accounts, each involved someone with a nationally known prophetic ministry. I say this to make the point that these are not examples that happened in remote places or with isolated frequency. I believe these examples to be an accurate representation of what is happening on a national scale. I spoke with many leaders who had similar stories of their own, which I was not able to include due to a lack of space. I believe we face a church-wide crisis, and it will worsen if we do not embrace the truth and turn from lies.

The truths in this book may make you uncomfortable or bring conviction. I know this because I was convicted as I wrote. I found the Holy Spirit's illumination of the truth most revealing in areas where I have failed to walk in the accuracy of His will. I repented and changed my outlook on giving words prefaced with "Thus saith the Lord."

It is my sincere hope that this book will focus and sharpen those already used in the realm of prophetic ministry. To accomplish this we must maintain an open and teachable heart. We must believe the truths read in God's Word instead of reading what we already believe. When confronted with truth we can respond two ways. We can become angry and defensive like Cain, the son of Adam, and forsake a revelation we need. Or we can be humble and broken like David when confronted by Nathan, and rise to a new level in godly character.

Teaching establishes us, but warnings protect us.

2

WIDESPREAD DECEPTION

W e presently live on the threshold of great change—the final years, days, and hours before our Lord's Second Coming. Most of you are already aware of this. Though Jesus said that we would not know the day or hour, He promised we would know the season—and it is upon us! Never before has such concurrent prophetic fulfillment occurred in the church, Israel, and nature. Jesus assured us that "this generation will not pass from the scene before all these things take place" (Matt. 24:34, NLT). These events will conclude with the Son of Man coming on the clouds of heaven to gather together His chosen from the far reaches of earth and heaven (Matt. 24:30–31).

Our time period is repeatedly mentioned throughout the Scriptures. It is quite possibly the most exciting as well as frightening time in the history of mankind. It's exciting because we stand to witness the greatest revelation of God's glory any generation has yet to experience. This will be accompanied by a harvest of souls of such magnitude it is unimaginable. It will be a time of great glory and joy.

Yet it will also be a time of judgment and fear, because we are explicitly told so by the apostle Paul. "But know this, that in the last days perilous times will come" (2 Tim. 3:1). These perilous times will be magnified by the spiritual darkness of widespread *deception.* This warning is repeatedly sounded throughout the New Testament. Each epistle echoed this message to the first-century church as an urgent warning for their day that was also to be passed on to the future generation of the last days.

This was not limited to the epistles. Jesus also warned of deception in the Gospels. In one such reference found in Matthew 24, four times He warned for us to beware of deception! When Jesus' disciples requested the signs that would precede His Coming, Jesus prefaced his response with, "Take heed that no one deceives you" (Matt. 24:4).

It is easy to sense the urgency of His words. There is a serious and solemn tone. Jesus wants His words ever before the disciples and imprinted on their souls. Two thousand years later, we would be wise not to neglect His warning.

God admonishes His own, "Hear, O my people, and I will warn you—if you would but listen to me, O Israel!" (Ps. 81:8, NIV). He is pleading with them, "I'm warning but you're not listening!" We only benefit from God's warning when we listen and heed His Word carefully. Parents know there are times when their children hear but do not heed what they say. When they are confronted they will often say, "But I did not understand what you meant." This is usually because they did not feel what we said was important enough at the time to ask questions or to figure out just how it applied to them. When there is a consequence, then they suddenly comprehend.

Just as with children and parents, it would be foolish for us to think we can handle God's warnings carelessly and remain free from consequence. Solomon realized this truth in his latter years, "Better a poor but wise youth than an old but foolish king who no longer knows how to take warning" (Eccles. 4:13, NIV). Solomon sought God's wisdom while a youth, and he enjoyed the blessings and benefits of God's wise counsel for a season. As a result the kingdom prospered and he lived a long and full life.

But as time passed he turned from the initial wisdom of his youth. It was not long before deception crept in. Though he possessed great knowledge and wisdom, he failed to heed it. Without this obedience or submission to truth, deception turned the feet of this brilliant king from the narrow path of righteousness unto the broad path of destruction. As his heart darkened, Solomon turned toward idolatry. All of his intelligence could not keep him from deception. So knowledge without corresponding obedience is as destructive as foolishness.

We are warned, "Let him who thinks he stands take heed lest he fall" (1 Cor. 10:12). To heed something means to give it special attention, consideration, and to be mindful of it. Its antonym is negligence. If our hearts are not guided by God's Word, we open ourselves up to destruction. Proverbs 28:26 says, "He who trusts in his own heart is a fool, but whoever walks wisely will be delivered." We cannot trust our hearts, because the Word of God tells us they are deceitful above all things (Jer. 17:9).

To walk wisely we must observe the whole counsel of the Word, not just portions. This includes the warnings. Proverbs 12:15 confirms that "he who heeds counsel is wise."

WARNINGS FOR THE CHURCH

Paul found it imperative to warn as well as teach. He instructed the stewards of the Word of God that both warning and teaching are necessary to present every person perfect in Christ. He wrote:

> Him [Jesus] we preach, warning every man and teaching every man in all wisdom, that we may present every man perfect in Christ Jesus.
>
> —COLOSSIANS 1:28

Teaching *establishes* us, but warnings *protect* us! If we are only taught, and the warnings are neglected, we can lose what was established through the ministry of teaching. This is true independent of how sound or great that teaching is. Solomon, the wisest and greatest teacher, turned when he did not heed God's warning. It does not matter how skillful we are in the Word of God; it can be perverted or destroyed when not accompanied by close attention to God's warnings.

In his final address to the elders of Ephesus, Paul emphasized again the importance of warning the sheep by using himself as an example.

> Therefore watch, and remember that for three years I did not cease to warn everyone night and day with tears.
> —ACTS 20:31

Notice it was continuous and for everyone, not just new converts.

It was so important that for three years Paul wouldn't allow a day to pass without warning them. Notice his passion as he reminded them of his tears. He wanted the image of a weeping father burnt into their memory. His heart cried with concern. Where are these fathers or shepherds today? Where are fathers who bear the burden of the sheep? These leaders refuse the comforts of today while they herald a warning for tomorrow. May God help us to have such hearts!

Today there is pressure on ministries to skirt controversial issues and make people feel comfortable. Too often this pressure is succumbed to in an effort to maintain and open new doors of opportunity for the "ministry." As a result, quite often healthy warnings are omitted in order not to jeopardize good offerings and invitations. While ministers' reputations may remain intact, the sheep are drawn away and torn by ravenous wolves because they lack the necessary protection.

TWO SOURCES OF DECEPTION

Jesus described two sources of deception: False christs, or antichrists, and false prophets. False christs, or antichrists, are those who deny that Jesus Christ, the Son of God, came in the flesh as a natural man. These deceivers have an antichrist spirit (1 John 2:18–23; 2 John 7–8). Historically they have maintained that Jesus was never really the son of man, that He was always divine and therefore never really died. Today this spirit manifests through various teachings of other cults. The bottom line is they always attack the truth of Jesus coming in the flesh. This thought line would be unacceptable in any scripturally based church or believer's life. It is not antichrists of which I warn you.

The second category of deceivers that Jesus defined is false prophets. These prophets can be further divided into two categories. First, there are those who proclaim another way to God, usually described as the Higher Power. They present a way to God that goes around Jesus Christ instead of through Him. Again, most believers would not give attention to these prophets. However, the second group of false prophets are harder to recognize. They are in the church, and if unchecked they can deceive even the elect. Jesus said these prophets will arise with signs and wonders "so as to mislead, if possible, even the elect" (Matt. 24:24, NAS). They are among us, carrying the same Bible, accompanied by supernatural gifts, yet they mislead by drawing people to themselves instead of to the heart and rule of God.

Again, this is made clear by Paul's continual warning to the Ephesian church:

> I know that after I leave, savage wolves will come in among you and will not spare the flock. Even from your own number men will arise and distort the truth in order to draw away disciples after them. So be on your guard! Remember that for three years I never stopped warning each of you night and day with tears.
>
> —ACTS 20:29–31, NIV

Notice Paul says they come as wolves. Jesus described these false prophets as wolves in sheep's clothing (Matt. 7:15). Notice He did not say shepherd's clothing; therefore they may or may not have a public ministry. It is important that we do not limit the *false prophet* to one in pulpit ministry. Jesus' emphasis was that from all appearances they will portray a believer, and their outward appearance would conceal their inward motive. All full-time pulpit ministers should be believers, yet not all believers are full-time pulpit ministers (Eph. 4:11). So Jesus' words show us that false prophets mix just as easily with the congregation as they do with the pulpit ministers.

False prophets resemble the believers. They can talk, teach, preach, sing, or act just like them. But their desire or motivation is entirely different. True believers delight in fulfilling the desires of their Master. Wolves think only of themselves. If obedience does not interfere with the fulfillment of their agenda they will submit, thereby making it difficult at times to distinguish them from believers. This is why Jesus said that they can only be identified by their fruit. True fruit remains constant through adverse circumstances and brings health and life to others.

False prophets are those who have yet to submit their lives to the lordship of Jesus. They have sought God for the wrong reasons. They serve Him for what they can get from Him rather than for who He is. They are impostors and easily mistaken until their motives are revealed. In fact, they not only deceive others, but they also deceive themselves (2 Tim. 3:13, see especially the New Century Version). They really believe they are living a life of obedience. On that final day, they are the ones who called Jesus *Lord* and prophesied in His name, only to hear Him say, "I never knew you; depart from Me, you who practice lawlessness [do not do the will of my Father]." (See Matthew 7:15–23.) This type of deception will be so effective that Paul still remained concerned that believers would be drawn away even after he warned them day and night for three years!

Paul shakes any confidence the Ephesians would have in themselves with his comment, "even from your own number" (the NKJV says, "from among yourselves . . . ") men will arise and distort the truth in order to draw away disciples after themselves (Acts 20:30, NIV). The New Living Translation is even more pointed: "Even some of you will distort the truth in order to draw a following."

These are believers who served and produced fruit in the past, but somewhere along the line something of their old nature sprang up, or perhaps they were led astray, so they turned to serve themselves again. Keep in mind Paul is addressing the elders of the church. What a thing to say to the very leaders he has poured himself into! This lends a greater understanding to his tears. How difficult it must have been for him. But the need superseded the difficulty. Today is no different. There has never been a greater need for truth because Jesus described these last days as breeding period for deception.

Today the church has been infiltrated with the counterfeit prophetic. As a result it has literally been polluted, even to the extent it has distorted the true Word of the Lord. The counterfeit is now more popular and readily accepted than the true. We must hear from heaven before corruption overtakes the church.

A WAKE-UP CALL

For almost the entire decade of the 1980s I served full time on staff in a local church. For the entire decade of the 1990s I have visited hundreds of churches of varying denominations located on every continent, as well as conferences and Bible schools. As a result I've seen and experienced both the wonderful and disheartening on local, national, and international levels. I believe God has allowed this that I might better serve His people.

My wife and I have experienced the counterfeit prophetic ministry firsthand. We have listened to numerous tales of abuse and walked with others through their encounters with counterfeit prophetic ministry. Cases have varied from the mildly detrimental to the disastrous. I've listened to pastors share how false divination destroyed families and controlled or split churches. I saw it in our local church. In some cases the deception is now evident, but only after the damage was done. More often than not these prophets continue on as before due to a lack of shepherding by the overseers of the church. Often these overseers are intimidated as well. Paul admonished leadership:

> Therefore take heed to yourselves and to all the flock, among which the Holy Spirit has made you overseers, to shepherd the church of God which He purchased with His own blood.
> —ACTS 20:28

A shepherd not only feeds; he also protects. It is time for the leaders to rise up and protect their flock. This means no longer overlooking or casually shrugging off false prophecies. I was so

15

blessed by the following commentary I read in a recent issue of *Ministries Today*.

> Last year while I was meeting with a group of Christian leaders, everyone started telling funny stories about false prophecies. As I listened and laughed, I saw that it had become common practice to ignore, or at least take lightly, many of the people "speaking in the name of the Lord." We had all learned to hold our tongues and be gracious. Everyone told of receiving notes, participating in meetings and actually encouraging people in prophetic words, knowing they were not genuine . . . "

This meeting left him searching for truth. After examining God's Word he wrote:

> I concluded that false prophesy is a misuse of the Lord's name—which is a violation of the third commandment—and that people's fragile egos need to take a little heat if they are proclaiming themselves to be God's spokesperson and are not![1]

This is an example of a pastor sounding an alarm to the body of Christ of the inherent dangers of false prophecy. It is part of shepherding the people of God.

We hear personal or corporate prophecies given in the name of the Lord. We sometimes gaze in amazement or weep at the accuracy of the word given. But then we don't realize the defilement that has transpired until the damage has already taken place, months or even years later.

In this book we will clearly see from the Scriptures as well as from experiences that line up with the Word of God that accuracy does not determine whether a word was from the Lord. In fact, a word can be extremely accurate and spoken as, "Thus says the Lord . . . ," and not be from the mouth of the Lord at all.

How do we know if we are being led or misled? The answer is clearly seen in the following verses:

The statutes of the LORD are right, rejoicing the heart; the commandment of the LORD is pure, enlightening the eyes; The fear of the LORD is clean, enduring forever; the judgments of the LORD are true and righteous altogether. More to be desired are they than gold, yea, than much fine gold; sweeter also than honey and the honeycomb. Moreover by them Your servant is warned, and in keeping them there is great reward.

—PSALM 19:8–11

When we fear the Lord we will be kept pure and clean and will be properly trained, taught, and warned by His Word. The reason two people can read the same Bible and one fall into the path of deception while the other is led into the ways of the Lord is simply because they differ in their fear of the Lord.

If you fear God you will heed the warnings from His Word. As you read, cry out from within your heart as the psalmist did, "Teach me your way, O LORD, and I will walk in your truth; give me an undivided heart, that I may fear your name" (Ps. 86:11, NIV).

The more readily we recognize
the real, the less vulnerable we
are to the false.

$$\underline{3}$$

THE TRUE PROPHETIC MINISTRY I

To properly identify the counterfeit we must first outline the real. A recent documentary on one of the major television networks exemplified this truth. It was reported to the news team that certain jewelry stores were selling man-made stones as real. These stores had been in business for years, and scores of men and women had purchased what they believed to be precious stones. These patrons not only bought stones for themselves, they also shared these treasures with others.

No one questioned the authenticity of the stones until individuals with trained eyes pointed out they were man made. The news teams went into the stores with hidden cameras and, after several weeks of investigation, exposed the scam.

How did these jewelers deceive so many? The answer is quite simple. The counterfeit looked remarkably like the real. The difference was not perceivable unless you had a trained eye. I watched as an expert in the field taught the anchorwoman how to identify the counterfeit. First, he established the criteria of the authentic. He showed her what a real stone looked like under the scrutiny of a high-powered magnifying glass. Then he explained what to look for in the counterfeit. Without this training she would just as easily have been deceived due to a lack of knowledge.

These same principles hold true for identifying the true or false prophetic. The more readily we recognize the real, the less vulnerable we are to the false. If I'd never seen a real sapphire or emerald, I could easily be deceived. You could give me a green stone and tell me it was a sapphire. I wouldn't know that sapphires are actually blue, so I would have no reason to doubt you. You could provide books outlining the characteristics of green sapphires to further this deception. In no time I would be resistant to the characteristics of the real. This explains how many are deceived by cults.

Conversely, if I knew that sapphires are blue, I would immediately reject any other color. Any counterfeit would have to at least look like a sapphire. I could still fall prey to any wily jeweler with a good imitation, as did the many who were taken by the jewelry stores of the news documentary. But what if I'd been trained? Then it would be almost impossible to deceive me, even with the best counterfeit.

We're told, "All Scripture is God-breathed and is useful for teaching, rebuking, correcting and training in righteousness" (2 Tim. 3:16, NIV). In the Word of God we find our necessary training and guidelines. The more skilled we become in the Scriptures, the more evident and clear the delineation becomes between true and false, right and wrong. The Word is our safeguard from deception.

All too often we are like the patrons of the jewelry store who spent their money on costly imitations. We possess only a surface knowledge of the genuine. We lack the wisdom to separate the precious from the worthless. Untrained eyes can easily mistake the imitation for the real. A counterfeit prophecy is often made to look genuine by tagging on a "thus saith the Lord . . . ," followed by sympathy over past hurts and the pronouncement of "blessings" yet to come. Then you're hooked.

PROPHET DEFINED

The first mention of the word *prophet* in Scripture is a reference to Abraham found in Genesis 20:7. God warned Abimelech, "Now therefore, restore the man's wife; for he is a prophet." When we think of Abraham, a prophet is not the first description that comes to mind. We don't think of him as one because we don't see him foretelling future events, yet God saw him as one. This exposes an immediate misconception or limitation we have of prophets. Let's allow the Scriptures to give the true description of a prophet.

In reference to Abraham, the Hebrew word for *prophet* is *nabi'*. This is the most common word used for prophet in the Old Testament, appearing more than three hundred times. When an author introduces a term he usually defines it—if not the first time, then shortly after. In this case, a clear definition of *prophet* is not given the first time that God—the author of the Scriptures—uses it. But we learn more about its meaning on the following occurrences.

The second occurrence of *nabi'* in Scripture gives a general overview of its meaning. In Exodus 7:1 we read:

> So the LORD said to Moses: "See, I have made you as God to Pharaoh, and Aaron your brother shall be your prophet."

The setting is immediately after Moses shared his inability to speak clearly and contended that he cannot appear before Pharaoh as God's spokesman (Exod. 4:10–16). Though this displeased God, He still appointed Aaron (Moses' older brother) as Moses' representative. He explained:

> So he shall be your *spokesman* to the people. And he himself shall be as a *mouth* for you, and you shall be to him as God.
> —EXODUS 4:16, EMPHASIS ADDED

From these two scriptures we can derive the overall definition of prophet. Moses had the message, but Aaron was the voice. God said that Aaron would be a prophet, or spokesman, for Moses. The definition of a prophet is found in its function: *A prophet is one who speaks for another, or one who lends his voice to another.* The concept of a prophet as a foreteller of the future is erroneous.

This basic definition of *nabi'* is supported again in its first occurrence of its reference to Jesus. God promised Moses that for His people He will "raise up for them a Prophet like you from among their brethren, and will put My words in His mouth, and He shall speak to them all that I command Him" (Deut. 18:18). This of course speaks of Jesus. Hebrews 1:1–2 reiterates the role of a prophet by saying, "God, who at various times and in various ways spoke in time past to the fathers by the prophets, has in these last days spoken to us by His Son." Again the emphasis is on being a representative or spokesman rather than a foreteller of events.

Jesus Himself confirmed this: "For I have not spoken on My own authority; but the Father who sent Me gave Me a command, what I should say and what I should speak" (John 12:49). The clearest definition of a *prophet* is "one who speaks for another." This could entail foretelling the future, but it is far from a true prophet's emphasis.

THE NEW TESTAMENT PROPHET

To further define a prophet we must examine what the New Testament has to say. Scripture records when Jesus rose from the dead that He set ministry gifts or offices in place for the purpose of building up and strengthening His church.

> And He Himself gave some to be apostles, some prophets, some evangelists, and some pastors and teachers, for the equipping of the saints for the work of ministry, for the edi-fying of the body of Christ, till we all come to the unity of the faith and of the knowledge of the Son of God, to a perfect man, to the measure of the stature of the fullness of Christ.
> —EPHESIANS 4:11–13

Notice that Jesus is the one who appoints these offices. A person does not choose to occupy one. It is a calling from God and must come through His appointment. We will discuss this in greater detail in chapter eleven.

Notice these offices are given until the body of Christ comes into the unity of the faith and knowledge of Jesus Christ. This has yet to occur and did not conclude with the passing of the apostles and prophets who penned the New Testament. Therefore, the office of prophet is still very much in place and necessary.

Though most would agree on this, it is still important to emphasize that present apostles or prophets no longer write or add to the Scriptures. The Book of Revelation warns that if anyone adds to the words of the Scriptures God will bring plagues on their life. And if anyone takes away from the words of the Bible, God shall remove his part from the Book of Life (Rev. 22:18–19). Therefore, anything now spoken must not in any way contradict established Scriptures. As Paul said, "If anyone preaches any other gospel to you than what you have received, let him be accursed" (Gal. 1:9).

On the other hand Peter gives us this exhortation, "Are you called to be a speaker? Then speak as though God himself were speaking through you" (1 Pet. 4:11, NLT). A prophet is one who has a message from God to His church. In illustration, look at the messengers of a king. The king either directly communicates with his people or by way of his appointed messengers. It is crucial that the messengers deliver accurately not only the words of the king, but also his heart. The messenger must convey the message as though the king himself were doing it.

Though a prophet's message must not contradict Scripture, at times he may bring a message that cannot be confirmed by chapter and verse. This can be a genuine word from God. A good example is the word Agabus gave to the church in Antioch of the great famine that would come on the earth (Acts 11:27–28), or his warning to Paul that the Jews would bind him and deliver him into the hands of the Gentiles (Acts 21:10–11). It is in these areas where the counterfeit can easily come into play. A false prophet can give an individual or group a message whose authenticity cannot be confirmed or reputed by Scripture. Often this message comes from their own inspiration or from familiar spirits. If not confronted, these messages or prophetic words can defile God's people and make them worthless (Jer. 23:16). Defilement will be explained in chapter five in detail. It is my prayer the truth in this book will warn, protect, or liberate you from this sort of defilement.

Let's examine what the Scriptures reveal about the prophetic ministry of these latter days.

ELIJAH THE PROPHET

Behold, I will send you Elijah the prophet before the coming
of the great and dreadful day of the LORD. And he will turn
the hearts of the fathers to the children, and the hearts of the
children to their fathers, lest I come and strike the earth with
a curse.

—MALACHI 4:5–6

The great and dreadful day of the Lord is the Second Coming of
Christ. Jesus said that on that day "all the tribes of the earth will
mourn, and they will see the Son of Man coming on the clouds of
heaven with power and great glory" (Matt. 24:30). It will be a terrible day for those who do not love and obey Him. John the
Apostle was given a vision of that day and described how they "hid
themselves in the caves and in the rocks of the mountains, and said
to the mountains and rocks, 'Fall on us and hide us from the face of
Him who sits on the throne and from the wrath of the Lamb! For
the great day of His wrath has come, and who is able to stand?'"
(Rev. 6:15–17).

Before this day comes, God will send Elijah the prophet. This
Elijah who is to come is not the Elijah of 1 and 2 Kings come back
to earth. The text is not referring to a historic man, nor is it limited
to a mere man. Rather, it describes the true meaning of Elijah. To
explain, the word *Elijah* comes from two Hebrew words: *el* and
Yahh, el meaning "strength or might" and *Yahh* being the sacred
and proper name for the one true God, Jehovah. By putting them
together we come up with "strength or might of Jehovah, the one
true God." So what Malachi was saying is that prior to the day of
the Lord, God would send a prophetic ministry in the strength and
might of the one true God.

Prior to Jesus' first coming, the angel Gabriel appeared to
Zacharias, the father of John the Baptist, and described the call
upon his son's life:

And he will turn many of the children of Israel to the Lord
their God. He will also go before Him [Jesus] in the spirit and

24

power of Elijah, "to turn the hearts of the fathers to the children," and the disobedient to the wisdom of the just, to make ready a people prepared for the Lord.

—Luke 1:16–17

John was a prophet sent in the spirit and power of Elijah to prepare the way of the Lord prior to Jesus' first coming. The thrust of his message and ministry was to turn the hearts of the children of Israel back to God. In doing this, their leaders would no longer serve themselves but the people, and the disobedient would return to submission to the Word or ways of God.

John's message can be summarized in one statement, "Repent, for the kingdom of heaven is at hand!" (Matt. 3:2). *Repentance* means a change of mind and heart, not just action. The children of Israel's actions were often spiritual or religious, while their hearts drifted from God. Thousands attended synagogues, all the while unaware of the true condition of their hearts. They trusted in the fact that they were descendants of God's covenant people. They were confident in their salvation and believed they were in good standing with God. Yet they were deceived!

In His mercy, God raised up the prophet John to expose their true heart condition by proclaiming the word of the Lord. "Here is a sample of John's preaching to the crowds that came for baptism: 'You brood of snakes! Who warned you to flee God's coming judgment? Prove by the way you live that you have really turned from your sins and turned to God. Don't just say, "We're safe—we're the descendants of Abraham." That proves nothing. God can change these stones here into children of Abraham'" (Luke 3:7–8, NLT).

It is interesting to note this was his message to the crowds who had traveled hours out into the scorching desert to hear his preaching and be baptized by him. These were not complacent city residents who mocked him and refused to be inconvenienced by a trek through the desert to hear him. John was not interested in being popular. He did not flatter those who came to his meetings; he burned with a passion to be faithful to declare what God spoke to him. He was a prophet in the truest sense. Yet this is a far cry from what we experience in ministry today.

THE ELIJAH ANOINTING TODAY

John the Baptist fulfilled the Elijah prophecies (there are others, such as Isa. 40:3–4; Mal. 3:1) prior to the Lord's first coming. However, Malachi prophesied this anointing would be sent prior to the great and dreadful day of the Lord—His Second Coming. This means there are two different fulfillments of the prophecy. Jesus spoke of these two fulfillments to three of His disciples.

Jesus took Peter, James, and John up to a high mountain. There He was transfigured before them. His face shone like the sun, and His clothes became radiant white. Moses and Elijah appeared and conversed with Jesus. While Jesus was speaking, a bright cloud overshadowed them and God spoke saying, "This is My beloved Son, in whom I am well pleased. Hear Him!" The fear of God overwhelmed the disciples, and they fell on their faces. When they looked up, they were alone with Jesus.

It was now very clear to them that Jesus was the long-awaited Messiah. However, this puzzled them. They had heard the scribes teach from the Book of Malachi that before the Lord came Elijah would come first. They asked Jesus about this, and His response was:

> "Indeed, Elijah is coming first and will restore all things. But I say to you that Elijah has come already, and they did not know him but did to him whatever they wished. Likewise the Son of Man is also about to suffer at their hands." Then the disciples understood that He spoke to them of John the Baptist.
>
> —MATTHEW 17:11–13

Jesus spoke of two separate Elijahs. First he spoke of the Elijah that is coming (future tense). This could not have been a reference to John since at that point he had already been beheaded (Matt. 14:1–12). Then Jesus spoke of the Elijah that had already come (past tense), which He clearly identified as John the Baptist.

Preceding the return of Jesus, God will again raise up a prophetic anointing. However, this time the mantle will not rest upon a single man but corporately on a group of prophets (Eph. 4:7–11; Rev. 22:8–9). These Elijah prophets will proclaim a message similar to John the Baptist's, for he was a type and forerunner of these latter-day prophets. They will seek out the lost or deceived sheep in the church, as well as call back those who have left from offense.

Many of the deceived even now attend church and feel they're ready for Jesus' return. Not unlike the multitude in John the Baptist's time, they comfort themselves with their church attendance, tithing record, ability to speak in tongues, or ability to flow in other gifts. They feel certain God is obligated to accept them because they once prayed a sinner's prayer, though they have yet to submit to the lordship of Jesus. They only obey when it is convenient or doesn't conflict with their schedule or agenda. If obedience to the Master interferes with their pleasure they casually ignore His leading, claiming "the grace of God." They may believe they are justified, but are they? Could they be the lukewarm church Jesus confronts in Revelation, which finds confidence in a false grace (Rev. 3:14–22)? Unfortunately, this condition is further propagated by false prophets and teachers who tell them they are in right standing with God.

Lukewarm messages have spawned a multitude of converts over the last few decades. But there are many who truly love and fear God, though they may have grown somewhat weary. They seem to be the minority and cannot understand where the true word of the Lord is that will pierce the heart of the church and again make it whole. The message of these Elijah prophets will strengthen those who have persevered in obedience in a troubled church. Their words will again bring clarity to the purposes of God for His End-Time church.

In the next chapter we'll examine more closely a true prophet's message and why it is so desperately needed today.

Telling people what they want
to hear at the expense of what
they need to hear weakens the
church.

4

THE TRUE PROPHETIC MINISTRY II

The last chapter established through the Scriptures that a prophet is a spokesperson for the Lord Jesus. We also learned about the role of the prophetic in the End Times.

> Behold, I will send you Elijah the prophet before the coming of the great and dreadful day of the LORD. And he will turn the hearts . . .
>
> —MALACHI 4:5–6

John the Baptist fulfilled the Elijah prophecy for his day and foreshadowed the type of prophetic anointing that would come forth prior to Jesus' Second Coming. John's purpose was to awaken the "lost sheep" of the house of Israel, to prepare them for Jesus' first coming. He was not sent to the heathen. The angel Gabriel described the focus of his ministry:

> And he will turn many of the children of Israel to the Lord their God.
>
> —LUKE 1:16

This corresponds with Malachi's description of the prophetic: to turn hearts back to the ways and wisdom of God. There is a common thread that runs through the message of nearly every prophet in the Bible. It represents the heartbeat of their call. Its emphasis could be summarized as: "Turn to the Lord with all your heart!" Though speaking in different tones, settings, and levels of intensity, each prophet burned with a passion to see God's people restored to Him that they might walk in His ways.

Let's examine a sampling of their words, which confirms this common chord.

MOSES

Return to the LORD your God and obey His voice, according to all that I command you today, you and your children, with all your heart and with all your soul.

—DEUTERONOMY 30:2

Moses' entire mission was to call and deliver God's people out of Egyptian bondage that they might experience the revelation of their God and serve Him.

SAMUEL

Then Samuel spoke to all the house of Israel, saying, "If you return to the LORD with all your hearts, then put away the foreign gods and the Ashtoreths from among you, and prepare your hearts for the LORD, and serve Him only; and He will deliver you from the hand of the Philistines."

—1 SAMUEL 7:3

ISAIAH

Return to Me, for I have redeemed you.

—ISAIAH 44:22

JEREMIAH

Before captivity:

"If you will return, O Israel," says the LORD, "Return to Me; and if you will put away your abominations out of My sight, then you shall not be moved."

—JEREMIAH 4:1

After captivity:

Let us . . . examine our ways, and turn back to the LORD.

—LAMENTATIONS 3:40

EZEKIEL

Therefore say to the house of Israel, "Thus says the Lord GOD: 'Repent, turn away from your idols, and turn your faces away from all your abominations.'"

—EZEKIEL 14:6

HOSEA

Come, and let us return to the LORD.

—HOSEA 6:1

JOEL

"Now, therefore," says the LORD, "turn to Me with all your heart."

—JOEL 2:12

AMOS

For thus says the LORD to the house of Israel: "Seek Me and live."

—AMOS 5:4

ZECHARIAH

Therefore say to them, "Thus says the LORD of hosts: 'Return to Me,' says the LORD of hosts, 'and I will return to you.'"
—ZECHARIAH 1:3

MALACHI

"Yet from the days of your fathers you have gone away from My ordinances and have not kept them. Return to Me, and I will return to you," says the LORD of hosts.
—MALACHI 3:7

ALL OTHER PROPHETS

Yet the LORD testified against Israel and against Judah, by all of His prophets, every seer, saying, "Turn from your evil ways, and keep My commandments and My statutes, according to all the law which I commanded your fathers, and which I sent to you by My servants the prophets."
—2 KINGS 17:13

The major thrust of these servants was to declare God's heart to His people, pricking their hearts that they might return to His ways. Notice this was the purpose of *all of His prophets* sent to Israel and Judah. In fulfilling this they may have spoken of things to come or given a personal word to an individual. However, these were *minor* components of their ministry, which helped to accomplish the *major*. Too often we are deceived or led astray by majoring on that on which God minors, while minoring on that on which God majors.

It would seem that the emphasis of today's prophetic ministries is focused on the *minor*, the giving of personal prophecy and foretelling of the future. We've drawn our definition of a prophet from limited and specific scriptures rather than stepping back to capture the overall picture. An erroneous view of a prophet has left the church vulnerable to deception. The counterfeit or incomplete becomes easier to embrace than the real.

As I travel throughout the United States and abroad, my heart is grieved as I listen to numerous pastors and believers treat those in the prophetic ministry as fortunetellers. I've had leaders question me before I minister, "Are you planning to give words to people after the service?" By their tone I knew they hoped my answer would be yes. They allude that other speakers have "moved in the prophetic," their people enjoyed it, and they want me to perform in some similar fashion. They offer to have individual tapes ready to record the words for their members.

Underneath this attitude is an assumption that I can turn the prophetic unction on and off as I please. They cite scripture that the spirit of a prophet is subject to the prophet (1 Cor. 14:32). Yet does that mean the prophet is no longer subject to the Holy Ghost? The messenger does not determine what he speaks; he is but a servant and a spokesperson. My Bible says the gift of prophecy operates "as He [the Spirit] wills," not as I will it (1 Cor. 12:11).

One pastor complained after I had conducted two Sunday services, "I don't know how many people will come back tomorrow since you didn't give anyone a personal prophecy." Has the Holy Spirit been reduced to a fortuneteller who performs in order to maintain a crowd? It just so happened that in these services God had told me to deal with insubordination. It was not a comfortable message to deliver nor to sit under. The pastor felt the tension and conflict of this and was uncomfortable. He was much more comfortable with prophetic ministries that came in and gave everyone encouraging words.

Within two years of the message God had me deliver on insubordination, one of his associate pastors, who was considered to be prophetic, split the church and left with many of the members to start a "new work" a little ways across town. This associate had received all sorts of positive words from previous "prophets" who had visited the church and prophets at outside conferences. Yet he had a heart like Absalom, David's son who rebelled against him. He broke his relationship with his pastor, whom he criticized openly. I returned to that church a few years later and ministered to the pastor, but I'm sad to say the damage had already been done.

Telling the people what they want to hear at the expense of what they need to hear weakens the church. It causes people to seek the gifts and manifestations to the neglect of pursuing the character of God.

The prophetic ministry God is raising up in these latter days will be after the order of John the Baptist. Their ministries will trumpet the same call and warning as his. These prophets will call for change; their primary mission will be turning the hearts of God's people back to their Father. Their messages will be accompanied by strong conviction. Often the words might not seem "nice." Their preaching will hit the hardened areas of our hearts as a hammer smashing upon a rock. They will command, rebuke, correct, and exhort with all authority, yet it all will flow from a heart filled with love for God and His people.

Their words will cut some right to the heart, acting as a sword that will pierce through the soul so that the motives of the heart might be revealed. Those who possess hearts filled with gain and greed will lash out against their words. Those who love the truth will find their hearts ablaze with the same passion.

These prophets will not seek the accolades or rewards of man. They will only desire to handle faithfully the truth that sets men free. They will not be bought, for they already know their Rewarder. Power, popularity, or money will not influence their words.

They are the Elijah prophets who will speak as the oracles of God. Alight with holy fire, their words will act as skillfully guided missiles targeting the hearts of men. Their styles and intensities may differ, yet they will all follow the same orders.

I have sat under such ministries; some loudly proclaimed while others were spoken in quieter tones. Some made me laugh, yet I was constantly aware of a conviction that held me pinned to my seat. Often I trembled, yet all the while my heart longed for Jesus. The common denominator was that their words were like arrows that hit the target of my heart. After service I could not wait to get alone and seek the Lord of the message. I had heard a call to holiness in a fresh new way.

"THUS SAITH THE LORD . . ."

We have mistakenly limited a prophet to one who gives prophecies, words of knowledge, and words of wisdom packaged the way charismatic circles are used to hearing them. On the contrary, it is quite possible for a prophet to walk into a service and never say one "thus saith the Lord. . . ." Yet his entire message could be prophetic words of wisdom and of knowledge! Often we are not discerning enough to recognize the prophetic if it is not delivered with a few "thus saith the Lord's" or rhymes mixed in. We rely on statements like, "I hear the Lord saying . . ." or "The Spirit of God says . . ." to be sure it is Him talking.

Yet there is no record of John the Baptist saying, "Thus saith the Lord . . . ," and it seems he forgot it was necessary to give encouraging personal prophecies along with his public address. He also neglected to familiarize himself with the public speaking style of the Pharisees. He gave prophetic words to two groups: tax collectors, "Collect no more than what is appointed for you," and soldiers, "Do not intimidate anyone or accuse falsely, and be content with your wages." What a far cry from today! In our meetings we hear words like, "Thus saith the Lord, 'I am bringing a husband to you, and he is going to have money in one hand and ministry in the other.'" Or, "God doesn't want you to work . . . He is just going to have people give money to you!" No, these are not fictional illustrations. They are actual words given in meetings to individuals I know personally. These words may have appealed to the individuals, but are they scriptural? Do they strengthen their walk with God? Or do they return their focus back on themselves?

John the Baptist didn't give nice personal prophecies prefaced with "thus saith the Lord. . . ." In fact, under today's definitions the church would have had a hard time placing John in a ministry office (Pharisees long to put people in categories). He might have possibly passed as an evangelist, but never a prophet. By limiting the prophetic office to what we typically experience in the church today or to the minors of foretelling of coming events or personal words, we can easily miss what God will bring through His Elijah prophets!

OLD OR NEW TESTAMENT PROPHET?

There are those who may say, "John the Baptist was an Old Testament prophet. His ministry does not apply to us today." If that is the case, then why didn't God add a fortieth book to the Old Testament and call it "John the Baptist"? Look at what Mark's Gospel has to say:

> The beginning of the gospel of Jesus Christ, the Son of God. As it is written in the Prophets: "Behold I send My messenger . . . "
>
> —MARK 1:1–2

The messenger was John the Baptist. His ministry is clearly defined as the beginning of the gospel of Jesus. He is found in all four Gospels. Jesus later made it absolutely clear by saying, "The law and the prophets were until John" (Luke 16:16).

Notice Jesus did not say, "The law and the prophets were until Myself." Again, in Matthew 11:12–13 Jesus says, "And from the days of John the Baptist until now the kingdom of heaven suffers violence, and the violent take it by force. For all the prophets and the law prophesied until John." Notice Jesus references the starting place of the kingdom of heaven with John's ministry.

You may now question, "How can you write that the prophetic ministry of the latter days will be patterned after John the Baptist? I thought New Testament prophecy is 'for edification, exhortation, and comfort'" (1 Cor. 14:3–4). In answer, let's return to the Scripture and see what God says about John's prophesying.

We find the greatest detail about John's prophesying in the Gospel of Luke. He addressed the multitudes who had come out to listen and be baptized as, "You brood of snakes! Who warned you to flee God's coming judgment?" (Luke 3:7, NLT). He then warned that if they did not bear fruits worthy of repentance they would be cut down and thrown into the fire. For he said Jesus was coming with His winnowing fan in His hand, and He'd thoroughly clean out His threshing floor, which represented the house of Israel (Luke 3:17). Would you call these prophetic words edifying? Do they exhort or bring comfort? Most would answer, "No way!" But look at how God assessed them:

> And with many other *exhortations* he preached to the people.
> —LUKE 3:18, EMPHASIS ADDED

God categorized John's prophesying or preaching as exhortation! That is not what we'd call exhortive preaching today. Isaiah also described John's prophesying, but he didn't call it *exhortive;* rather, he called it *comforting!* He wrote:

> "Comfort, yes, comfort My people!" says your God. "Speak comfort to Jerusalem, and cry out to her . . ." The voice of one crying in the wilderness: "Prepare the way of the LORD; make straight in the desert a highway for our God."
> —ISAIAH 40:1–3

Do you think it is possible that we have had a warped view of edification, exhortation, and comfort? If you need further confirmation, look at Jesus' prophetic messages to the seven churches in Revelation 2 and 3! He warned one church that if they did not repent He would vomit them out of His mouth (Rev. 3:16)! How many would consider that prophecy comforting?

He described another church, "I know your works, that you have a name that you are alive, but you are dead" (Rev. 3:1). How many would find these words edifying? He went on to say, "I have not found your works perfect before God. . . . Therefore if you will not watch, I will come upon you as a thief" (Rev. 3:2–3). Do Jesus' words match our present view of prophetic ministry?

To another church He said, "Remember therefore from where you have fallen; repent and do the first works, or else I will come to you quickly and remove your lampstand from its place—unless you repent" (Rev. 2:5). The lampstand represented the church. To remove it from its place was to remove it from His presence. If they did not repent they would keep having their services, prayer meetings, prophetic conferences, and so on, yet His holy presence would have departed.

After commending two other churches for their service, He quickly warned one, "But I have a few things against you" (Rev. 2:14); then He proceeded to correct them. To the other church He added, "Nevertheless I have a few things against you," and corrected them (Rev. 2:20).

These are five of the seven prophecies given to seven churches. These messages were not just historic but have application to the church prior to the coming of the Lord Jesus Christ. Very little of what is happening in our prophetic conferences, meetings, or services today even remotely correlates with Jesus' or John the Baptist's pattern of prophecy. Could it be we've followed another pattern? Have we become like the prophets in the days of Jeremiah and Ezekiel, who prophesied peace and prosperity while God endeavored to call His people back to His heart?

The true prophetic word of God will build and strengthen us to stand against the storms of life. Counterfeit or soulish prophetic teaching or prophesying builds lives also, but it builds them on an unsure foundation.

5

PROPHETIC POLLUTION

While in prayer a few years ago I asked, "Lord, what is Your word for the church?" Immediately I heard the Holy Spirit say, "Jeremiah 23:11." I was not certain of the content of this passage, so I turned to it and found:

> "For both prophet and priest are profane; yes, in My house I have found their wickedness," says the LORD.

I was puzzled as I pondered this for a few moments, but I must admit with some embarrassment that I did not further inquire of the Lord for His specific message in this verse. Because I didn't understand it, I reasoned that perhaps I had not heard from God. So I left it alone and went on to other matters that immediately faced me in prayer.

About a month later, again while in prayer I asked the Lord the same question. Again I heard, "Jeremiah 23:11." Though I had not forgotten what had transpired a month earlier, I didn't recognize the reference. When I turned again to the passage, I was surprised to see it was the same one He had given me a month earlier. Because this was the second time, I took more notice. I read the entire chapter through and studied some of the Hebrew words of that particular verse, but again I failed to seek diligently the Lord's counsel in it. I did not wait to find out exactly what His message was.

Weeks passed, and again while in prayer I heard the Spirit of God say, "Read Jeremiah 23:11." This time I recognized the reference. I thought, *I think this is the very same scripture.* This time when I turned to it. I trembled as I read the words. From that moment forth I began to seek God diligently to know what He wants to communicate to us through this prophet's words.

Both Prophet and Priest Profane

I realized the entire twenty-third chapter of Jeremiah dealt with the counterfeit prophetic ministry. Even though Jeremiah was addressing Israel, his words hold a prophetic warning for our day as well. This was confirmed by his words, "In the last days you will clearly understand it" (Jer. 23:20, NAS). As we saw with the Elijah prophecies, this is another example of scriptures that have more than one fulfillment.

Jeremiah began his message with, "My heart within me is broken because of the prophets . . . " (v. 9). The prophets to whom he referred were not those of a false god or idol. No, these were prophets of Israel, the very ones who spoke in the name of Jehovah. They were well known and accepted among the assembly of believers, yet God lamented, "In My house I have found their wickedness" (v. 11). This caused Jeremiah's heart to break.

Is it different today? No, those with an understanding of the true prophetic can easily relate to his sorrow. It is not the false divining prophets who read palms, tarot cards, or speak by the stars that deeply grieve those hungry to see God glorified. Rather it is those who minister in Jesus' name in our churches and conferences who break the heart of the righteous. They are grieved because though the ministry is done in His name, it is not by His Spirit.

We must ask, "What did Jeremiah see that grieved him so deeply?" The answer is found in the scripture the Lord repeatedly pointed out to me: "For both prophet and priest are profane."

To understand we must go to the original language to grasp with greater clarity the meaning of *profane.* It is the Hebrew word *chaneph,* and it is defined as "to be profaned, defiled, polluted or corrupted." It appears ten times in the Old Testament, and only once is it translated "profane" in the New King James Version. Most often it is translated as "polluted" or "defiled." These two words best describe its meaning.

To pollute or defile something is to make what was once pure an ill mixture. As an example, five gallons of pure water is good for drinking, cooking, or bathing. But if you add a quart of hydrochloric acid, it becomes unusable. Even though the majority of the liquid—over 95 percent—is still water, there is not one ounce of the mixture that remains fit for consumption. The small percentage of acid corrupted the entire amount of water. The original five gallons of water now has become deadly to drink, toxic to cook with, and damaging to bathe in. It is important to note this sobering fact: The acid is undetectable by sight alone, for the mixture still appears to be pure water.

Jeremiah said, "The [prophets] follow an evil course and use their power unjustly" (v. 10, NIV). The power or gifting God gave them was polluted. Again, often it is difficult to discern the impurity of their gift! The prophet Ezekiel was also told to speak against many of the prophets of the Lord. His words help to clarify Jeremiah's statement:

> And the word of the LORD came to me, saying, "Son of man,
> prophesy against the prophets of Israel who prophesy . . . "
> —EZEKIEL 13:1–2

Notice God's message through Ezekiel was for the prophets of Israel, not the prophets of Baal or some other occultic worship. These prophets prophesied in the name of the Lord. Today in the current prophetic wave there is a lot of prophesying going on! These frequent words cover a wide range of matters. But is all of it truly God inspired? We find there was a mix in Ezekiel and Jeremiah's day:

> . . . and say to those who prophesy out of their own heart,
> "Hear the word of the LORD!"
> —EZEKIEL 13:2

Notice God explained that these prophets prophesied out of their own heart. In my New King James Bible the word *heart* has a reference marker by it. The corresponding note in the center column explains the word can also be translated *inspiration*. The New American Standard Version relays the passage this way: "Say to those who prophesy from their own *inspiration*, 'Listen to the word of the LORD!'" (emphasis added). So notice, they were prophesying by inspiration, but it was of their own making. It was not the inspiration of the Lord.

THE DANGER OF POLLUTED PROPHECY

This is but one of so many examples I could give, but this one poignantly illustrates this principle. It happened a few years ago, on a Sunday morning, during the first of a series of meetings held in a church on the West Coast.

It was my first time to this city. I'd only spoken briefly with the pastor twice, once by phone and later when he picked me up at the airport. I've made it a policy not to discuss church matters before ministering. I do this to keep from being influenced one way or another incorrectly. This makes it easier to remain sensitive to the Spirit of God. I had done this with this pastor and his associate also.

As I prepared for the first service I planned to speak along the lines of what I normally do on Sunday mornings. I'm usually drawn to the lost in the church—those who confess to be believers but still live for themselves. Yet that morning during worship I felt an uneasiness in my spirit. I sensed something amiss in this church's spiritual climate. I recognized it as what I come up against when divination or the counterfeit prophetic ministry has influence over a church. I sensed something had been released against this church.

Repeatedly I heard God say, "Deal with the error."

I asked for direction, "Where do I begin?"

I heard the Lord say, "Begin by reading Ezekiel 13."

After being introduced, I immediately instructed the congregation to turn to Ezekiel 13 and began to preach from that chapter. I confronted the counterfeit prophetic ministry that is sweeping through the church unchecked today. I shared how these prophets are speaking under inspiration, yet it is not the inspiration of the Holy Spirit. As I preached, I was aware that a stronghold in their thinking was being confronted. I also noticed the leadership was listening intently.

After service, I went to lunch with the pastor and his wife. As soon as we were alone, the pastor shared, "We needed this so much. You don't realize how on target you were this morning."

I responded, "Tell me. I am not used to preaching along this line on a Sunday morning service."

He went into great detail. "We had a prophet come into our church to minister, and the fruit was devastating. Let me tell you of a situation that occurred with a couple in our church."

He went on to share a tragic story of a couple in his church whose greatest desire was to work for an internationally known evangelist on the East Coast. The desire was strongest with his wife. Any time the evangelist was anywhere near they both attended every meeting they could, hoping to hook up with him.

Their pastor had invited a prophet to minister to the congregation. This man had never been to this church before and was unaware of any personal situations or desires within its body.

During the course of the service, he picked out this couple and asked them to stand up while he gave them a "word from God." His message went something like this, "Thus saith the Lord, 'I've called you to the ministry of healing. I am going to remove you from this fellowship and send you to the East Coast. There you will serve and be mentored by (at this point he named the evangelist they had desired to be with by name). He will pour himself into you, and it is there I will equip you for the healing ministry and bring his mantle upon you. Then after a season he will launch you, and I will bring you back to this part of the country where you will establish a powerful healing ministry.'"

The pastor said, "John, the couple was weeping with joy and amazement. Those in our congregation who knew they desired to work for this evangelist either wept along with them or stared in amazement at the accuracy of this word. Almost everyone in our fellowship was excited except my wife and me. We knew something was wrong."

Why? Because the pastor and his wife knew this couple well. They had sat with them through several sessions for marriage counseling. They were also concerned that this couple was overly enamored with ministry. They were not drawn to minister to people as much as they were drawn to the spotlight they saw coming with it.

The pastor shared how this couple began to pursue actively a position with this ministry. The husband finally quit his job, and they left for the East Coast. They met with one of the evangelist's right-hand men and shared what God had put on their hearts and their desire to serve the ministry in any capacity necessary.

The assistant thanked them, but no position was offered. So they waited for a door to open. After a period of time and after great disappointment the couple returned home. Nothing at all had happened. They spent a good portion of an inheritance they had received attempting to make ends meet, and they eventually lost their house.

The pastor looked at me and said, "Do you want to know what I believe happened?"

I said, "Yes!"

He said, "I believe this man came in and read the desires of their heart and spoke those desires out with the label of 'thus saith the Lord. . . .' But it was not what God was saying at all."

I agreed with him and said, "I have seen this happen frequently in the church, and that is exactly what I was speaking about this morning."

Recently the pastor informed me this couple is now divorced. The wife lives on the East Coast and works in some kind of ministry, not at all connected with the evangelist, while the devastated husband still lives on the West Coast.

The words spoken over this couple were spoken as if they were the Lord's words for them, yet they were not. God's message would have been altogether different. It would have brought the healing truth they needed to hear, not merely a reflection of their own desires. God continued through Ezekiel:

> You say, "The LORD says," but I have not spoken.
> —EZEKIEL 13:7

To say "the Lord says" when God has not spoken is a blatant lack of the fear of the Lord. It violates the third commandment,

> You shall not take the name of the LORD your God in vain, for the LORD will not hold him guiltless who takes His name in vain.
>
> —EXODUS 20:7

God rebuked these profane prophets through Jeremiah:

> I have not spoken to them, yet they prophesied.
>
> —JEREMIAH 23:21

DISCERNMENT (THE PROPHETIC GIFTING)

The story of this couple is one of numerous incidents I've heard or encountered; I'm sure you could add your own. We must now ask, "How could this minister have been so accurate with this couple, yet still be so wrong?" The answer is not as complicated as some would think. First, realize that we are spirit beings, and we can develop the ability to perceive the souls of others and read them. This ability is a form of discernment. If there is a call on our lives to prophetic ministry, then the ability to discern people's hearts will be even stronger.

Paul told how the pure gift of prophecy discerns men's lives. He said if we are prophesying and someone comes into the service whose heart is not right with God, "they will be convicted of sin." He then said, "As they listen, their secret thoughts will be laid bare, and they will fall down on their knees and worship God" (1 Cor. 14:24–25, NLT). The prophetic gifting carries with it the ability to lay bare the thoughts of men.

This is not to say that discernment sees only sin. It will recognize godly characteristics in people's lives as well. Philip brought a man named Nathanael to Jesus. As they approached, Jesus said, "Here comes an honest man—a true son of Israel." This amazed Nathanael, so he asked, "How do you know about me?" Jesus replied, "I could see you under the fig tree before Philip found you"

(John 1:45–48, NLT). Jesus was not merely referring to seeing Nathanael physically under the tree. Rather, it was then that He glimpsed his heart and soul through discernment.

Paul says, "But he who is spiritual judges all things" (1 Cor. 2:15). The Greek word for judges is *anakrino*. Strong's dictionary of Greek words defines this as: "to scrutinize, investigate, interrogate, determine." Simply put, *anakrino* means "to examine closely." We understand this in terms of natural things. But Paul is not referring to an intellectual examination. For he says, "From now on, we regard no one according to the flesh" (2 Cor. 5:16). We are admonished to develop our spiritual senses. The Bible defines spiritually developed persons as those who, "by reason of use have their senses exercised to discern both good and evil" (Heb. 5:14). Jesus was so strong in His ability to discern the thoughts and intents of others that He did not entrust Himself to people, "because He knew all men, and had no need that anyone should testify of man, for He knew what was in man" (John 2:24–25).

This prophetic gifting, or discernment, can easily be polluted. Then the gift still operates, but it is a mix. Now instead of representing God's heart to the people and calling them to His ways, the person with the gifting reads their souls by discernment and tells them what they want to hear. Why would ministers operate in this way? The answer is simple. They want the approval or reward of man. They want something from those to whom they minister or those who stand by and witness it. This could mean a generous offering, acceptance, influence, or validation of their ministry. Bottom line, there is a hidden agenda. The ministers may not even realize their motives are carnal. We will discuss this in greater detail in chapter thirteen.

If the man who ministered to the couple on the West Coast had truly heard the voice of God, his message would have pierced through the soulish veil of this couple's desires and seen the obstacles in their heart. It would not even have been necessary for him to call them out (which often fuels the desire for personal attention) and preface his words with "Thus saith the Lord. . . ." The prophetic preaching of God's Word would have pierced through their infatuation with ministry and planted a seed of truth that, if accepted, would have healed their marriage. Though they not only accepted but acted on the exciting word that was given, it ultimately led them into destruction and divorce. The true Word of God brings to light hidden motives and convicts us of selfish ambition, strife, and envy in our lives, which ultimately brings healing. God lamented through Jeremiah:

> I have not spoken to them, yet they prophesied. But if they had stood in My counsel, and had caused My people to hear My words, then they would have turned them from their evil way and from the evil of their doings.
>
> —JEREMIAH 23:21–22

UNCOVERING THE TRUE FOUNDATION

This couple may have *wanted* to hear a word about ministry, but they *needed* to hear the proclaimed word of God. "For the word of God is living and powerful, and sharper than any two-edged sword, piercing even to the division of soul and spirit, and of joints and marrow, and is a discerner of the thoughts and intents of the heart. And there is no creature hidden from His sight, but all things are naked and open to the eyes of Him to whom we must give account" (Heb. 4:12–13).

Notice in these verses the Word of God is referred to as *His* not *its*. Jesus is the living Word of God, and nothing is hidden from His sight (Rev. 19:12–13). This husband and wife were excited about ministry. They traveled to hear great ministers and volunteered in services. By all outward appearances they seemed to be on fire for God. Only their pastor knew differently, that under the surface there was strife and self-seeking. On the surface they possessed a zeal for ministry; however, the motive or foundation of their hearts was hidden from the eyes of men, but not from the living Word of God.

True prophecy, when Jesus speaks, is as sharp as a double-edged sword. One edge severs and separates the holy from the unholy. Simeon spoke such a word to Mary and Joseph as they brought the baby Jesus to the temple on the eighth day. He confirmed the living

Word of God they held in their arms with these words: "Yes, a sword will pierce through your own soul also." For what reason would the sword pass not only through their souls but also all with whom their Son Jesus came in contact? It was so "that the thoughts of many hearts may be revealed" (Luke 2:35). Thoughts of the heart are not revealed to embarrass us but to deliver us from the hindrances that weaken our obedience to God.

The second edge of the sword brings healing and strength to guard against the snares of the enemy. In the Book of Revelation, as you examine the prophetic messages Jesus spoke to the churches in Asia you'll notice that each time He spoke a word of correction He followed it with words with which their place in the body of Christ could be rebuilt. This brings the necessary healing that truly builds us in righteousness.

God's call to Jeremiah exemplifies the calling of a prophet.

> Then the LORD put forth His hand and touched my mouth, and the LORD said to me: "Behold, I have put My words in your mouth. See, I have this day set you over the nations and over the kingdoms, to root out and to pull down, to destroy and to throw down, to build and to plant."
> —JEREMIAH 1:9–10

First the sword passes to root out, pull down, destroy, and throw down. But in the wake of the destruction of lies, God intends to build and plant. He destroys in anticipation of building anew. Before you can build a house, the land must be cleared. Before you can plant a field, its fallow ground must be broken. The second edge of His prophetic sword prepares a proper foundation. Paul said to the Ephesians, "So now, brethren, I commend you to God and to the word of His grace, which is able to build you up" (Acts 20:32). The Scriptures frequently compare our lives to the process of building. Paul says, "You are God's building." Then he warns, "But let each one take heed how he builds" (1 Cor. 3:9–10). The true prophetic word of God will build and strengthen us to stand against the storms of life (Matt. 7:24–27).

Counterfeit or soulish prophetic teaching or prophesying builds lives also, but it builds them on an unsure foundation. It strengthens areas that will eventually weaken us later. It appeals to the flesh and pride of man because it awards us the lusts or desires of our carnal nature. It places lives on an unprepared or unstable foundation and then constructs a building with the wrong materials—that which the world pursues. Instead of a piercing sword that cuts away and then heals and strengthens, these words satisfy the wrong motives of the people's hearts. God charged the false prophets:

> Because they have seduced My people, saying, "Peace!" when there is no peace—and one builds a wall, and they plaster it with untempered mortar . . .
>
> —EZEKIEL 13:10

It is interesting to note Jesus said, "Do not think that I came to bring peace on earth. I did not come to bring peace but a sword" (Matt. 10:34). The prophets of Ezekiel's day promised the very peace and prosperity unbelievers pursue. Their words did not confront their audiences with righteousness but instead lulled them into a stupor of false hope and comfort. But this comfort is only temporary, for Jesus promised His sword would separate flesh from spirit. This makes us healthy and whole from an eternal perspective.

God warned that receiving these seductive and pleasant words was comparable to building walls with untempered mortar. Webster's dictionary defines *untempered* as "not durable or strong." It cannot endure the test. These types of words do not give the people the strength they need to stand during the storms of life.

The Bible declares, "Every word of God is tested" (Prov. 30:5, NAS). God's Word has already passed the test. It supplies true strength in the face of adversity or corruption. It equips us for tests, trials, and tribulations to come. It empowers us to wage a good war in our fight against sin and depravity. Paul admonished Timothy:

> This charge I commit to you, son Timothy, according to the prophecies previously made concerning you, that by them you

may wage the good warfare, having faith and a good conscience, which some having rejected, concerning the faith
have suffered shipwreck.

—1 TIMOTHY 1:18–19

The warfare is not the battle for your new house or car promised
in a prophetic word. Nor is it the fight to see any other self-serving
desires fulfilled. No, it is the fight to maintain faith and a good
conscience toward God and man. It is the fight to see His kingdom
advanced. Prophecy should direct our hearts toward God and His
ways, not feed our fleshly desires and make us feel good.

This couple was promised a great ministry together. These words
encouraged them in their present condition. Yet the fruit of it tore
them out from under the true authority of God at their home
church, which could have protected them. They suffered a substantial financial loss, they lost their home, and worst of all they lost
their marriage. How tragic! God warned us through Ezekiel:

Say to those who plaster it with untempered mortar, that it
will fall. There will be flooding rain, and you, O great hail-
stones, shall fall; and a stormy wind shall tear it down. Surely,
when the wall has fallen, will it not be said to you, "Where is
the mortar with which you plastered it?"

—EZEKIEL 13:11–12

An encounter with a true word of the Lord gives the recipient
the opportunity to hear and embrace the truth. This is the true edification, exhortation, and comfort that build enduring strength.
The storms of life and the test of time will reveal the quality of construction in the life of each believer. God says after the storm the
walls of a person's life built with untested or untempered mortar
will be gone, "so that its foundation will be uncovered" (Ezek.
13:14).

Too often I've seen men and women like this couple. They have
a passion for ministry or the blessings of God. They love to sit
under preaching or prophesying that feeds their excitement. But a
storm will reveal that their foundation is faulty. They've erected

their lives on falsehoods. They've built on weak and untested words. What our nation needs is the prophetic word of God that pierces and reveals the true motives of men's hearts. By uncovering the hidden we can then be strengthened by the true, tested word of God.

To become familiar with authentic personal prophecy we need to return to the Scriptures for insight.

6

PERSONAL PROPHECY

Personal prophecy has become increasingly popular in recent years. The typical pattern for today's personal prophecy begins with the prophetic minister's revelation of a situation or event that has occurred or is now present in the individual's life. Frequently it tends to be past hurts or rejection. This is usually followed by a declaration of blessings or the promise of what God is going to do in the future. Not all are alike, but this is a common format. The term used frequently to describe a personal prophecy is "a word." Therefore it is common to hear someone say, "He had a word for me." Or, "Did you get a word?"

The individual giving these words may be a prophet or another believer. The propagation in recent years of personal prophecies has propelled many ministries to national recognition. Many of these prophets and prophetesses not only give prophetic words but also teach others how to do the same through seminars, books, tapes, or conferences. For the price of registration and a couple of sessions on a weekend you can become a prophet, or at least learn to prophesy at will. At most prophecy meetings individual short-length audio tapes are often prepared so the people can take home their personal words.

It is sad, but because we so desperately hunger for the supernatural and for the true prophetic, many have not exercised spiritual judgment as they have recklessly embraced all forms of this ministry. Jesus made it clear, "See to it that no one misleads you" (Matt. 24:4, NAS). The responsibility is ours!

We need to ask, "Why are so many easily led astray by personal prophecies that are not genuine?" First, often we are ignorant of the authentic. To become familiar with authentic personal prophecy, we need to return to the Scriptures for insight. Specifically, I want to review the New Testament personal prophecies. Since there are only a few compared to the Old Testament, we will cover all of the major ones.

Simon and Andrew

Jesus walked by their boat and said, "Follow Me, and I will make you fishers of men."

He did not say, "Follow Me, and I will give you joy and happiness. Nor did He say, "I will make you rich and prosperous." Why? Because Jesus never used the blessings or benefits of the kingdom to entice His followers to obedience. There was no promise of personal achievement or success—just the promise He'd make them servants (Matt. 4:18–19).

James and John

James and John came to Jesus asking for Him to grant them the privilege of sitting on His left and right hand in glory. Jesus then asked them if they were able to drink the cup that He would drink and be baptized with the baptism He was being baptized with. With confidence they said, "We are able."

So Jesus prophesied to them these words, "You will indeed drink the cup that I drink, and with the baptism I am baptized with you will be baptized; but to sit on My right hand and on My left is not Mine to give, but it is for those for whom it is prepared" (Mark 10:39–40).

The cup and the baptism He spoke of represented the sufferings He would face in Jerusalem (Matt. 26:42; Luke 12:50; John 12:23–27). He prophesied that they would suffer as He had suffered. This was not a pleasant promise or word for these two enthusiastic inquirers. They did not hear what they had hoped to hear. In fact, while looking excitedly for a privilege they received a pronouncement that would grip their hearts and sober their minds. They were told they had asked the wrong person, and then they were promised suffering (Mark 10:35–40; Matt. 20:20–23).

Simon Peter

Jesus told Simon Peter, "Satan has asked to have all of you, to sift you like wheat." Then the Lord said, "But I have pleaded in prayer for you, Simon, that your faith should not fail. So when you have repented and turned to me again, strengthen and build up your brothers" (Luke 22:31, NLT).

Notice Jesus did not say, "Peter, I am telling you the Father will not permit this. And I hear Him saying, 'I will cause you to come through this in great victory, and all will know of your great love for the Father and for His Son. And from this your ministry will spring forth to the nations. You will be a leader of leaders, and I will speak to the those with money to give to your ministry, and you will enjoy an abundance of finances to do this great work I have called you to do . . . ' Hallelujah!"

This would have been a great word, but it would not have been what God was saying! It would not have strengthened him to stand during hardship. Even though Peter did become a leader of leaders and people did lay money at his feet for the poor, it was not the focus of any prophetic word Jesus gave to him.

After Jesus prophesied his denial, Peter countered by affirming his commitment, but Jesus answered his passionate promise of loyalty with, "Peter, let me tell you something. The rooster will not crow tomorrow morning until you have denied three times that you even know me" (Luke 22:34, NLT).

What a strong prophetic word! Why didn't Jesus say, "Peter, My Father says, 'You are the most faithful of all my disciples.' I know you would never turn from Me"?

A second prophecy to Simon Peter

After His resurrection, Jesus again had a word for Simon Peter. It went like this: "The truth is, when you were young, you were able to do as you liked and go wherever you wanted to. But when you are old, you will stretch out your hands, and others will direct you and take you where you don't want to go." Jesus said this to let him know what kind of death he would die to glorify God. Then Jesus told him, "Follow me" (John 21:18–19, NLT).

Notice Jesus did not bring up Peter's past. He didn't say, "Peter, when you were younger you were abused and mistreated by your parents. Pastors and friends rejected you. But now I say to you, I will heal those scars and yes, bring you to a place of authority so that those who mistreated you will apologize and then serve your international ministry. And yes, you will live free from hardships for all you had to endure from childhood. Hallelujah!"

A church member named Sapphira

A personal prophecy was given to a church member named Sapphira after she and her husband conspired and lied to the Holy Spirit. Peter said to her, "How is it that you have agreed together to test the Spirit of the Lord? Look, the feet of those who have buried your husband are at the door, and they will carry you out" (Acts 5:1–11).

Notice Peter did not say, "And the Lord says, 'You are my daughter, and I am the God of a second chance! Do you want to rethink what you said? I know you didn't mean it.'"

Paul the Apostle

A personal prophecy was given to Paul at Tyre. The prophet Agabus came and took Paul's belt, bound his hands and feet, and said, "Thus says the Holy Spirit, 'So shall the Jews at Jerusalem bind the man who owns this belt, and deliver him into the hands of the Gentiles'" (Acts 21:10–11).

Notice Agabus did not say, "Thus says the Holy Spirit, 'There are those who would try to hinder your ministry in Jerusalem, but I will raise up a standard against them and personally keep them from bringing you into chains or imprisonment.'"

THE NEW TESTAMENT PATTERN

These New Testament prophecies that you just read do not follow

58

the pattern or content of the words we hear so often today. These days you can attend what many call "prophetic meetings or conferences." In some of these meetings numerous people are called out and given personal words. Most frequently they are prefaced with, "Thus saith the Lord . . ." or, "I hear the Lord saying . . ." or, "God says . . . " and so on. Yet are all these words straight from God's mouth when most follow a completely different pattern than what was set forth in the Scriptures?

When someone spoke prophetically in the New Testament, it was often to bring correction to people who had veered off course. Or if their lives were on target, the prophetic words strengthened them for battles or hardships ahead. This is why Paul encouraged Timothy to wage a good warfare with the prophesies that had been given to him (1 Tim. 1:18). Timothy had a pure heart and his life was on target. He was armed with the prophetic when he faced hardship or battles. This was also true with Paul when he received a prophetic word from Agabus. The prophetic word strengthened Paul's position to the place where he could say, "I am ready not only to be bound, but also to die at Jerusalem for the name of the Lord Jesus" (Acts 21:13).

Other times, prophetic words were given to impart gifts or to set apart believers for ministry. These *words* came from tested and tried overseers who labored among the believers and knew their lives—not from prophets who knew very little or nothing about their lives (1 Tim. 5:22, NCV; Acts 13:1–4). The Bible is clear about this. Paul writes that before a person can be brought into an office of serving he must first be tested! Only ministers who have watched the candidates' lives can do this, not strangers. For this reason Paul says, "Never be in a hurry about appointing an elder" (1 Tim. 5:22, NLT). We will discuss this in chapter eleven.

Today most prophecies to individuals seem to build up self and emphasize money, relationships, marriage, business, babies, or ministry. When I say ministry, it is nothing like what we read in the above passages. The words given most always seem to tell how exhilarating the call will be, or how greatly God will use them, or how important they are or will be. Then we have words that are given to individuals relating to leadership positions by "prophets" who know nothing about the individual's life.

Let's look at some actual words given to individuals. Keep in mind what we have seen in the Scriptures as you read these words represented as "straight from God's mouth."

A COUNTRY-CLUB ANOINTING?

One young man we know personally asked me to listen to a tape of a word he had been given by a well-known prophet. It began with him being told he would be a prophet of the Lord and would take a people and train them in the prophetic. The following is an exact transcript of the rest:

> I see you in a country club, tennis-court type of setting. And the Lord said He is going to open that whole realm, and He will send you through that door to minister to a country-club crowd. The Lord says you will not be able to be bought or sold, for the Lord is going to give you an independent wealth that shall cause you to remain independent from covetousness that many have fallen into. The Lord will build up under you a machine that will make money—a money-making machine—an organization and an ability to generate finances that will generate and actually evolve into an independent wealth. But the Lord reminds you, He will do this that you might remember that no man remembers the words of a poor wise man. "So I will take you and remove you from being poor so that wealthy men will listen. At first they will not listen because of your wisdom, but because of your stature and because of your lifestyle and because of the wealth that I have brought to you," says the Lord. "I have anointed you in the ability to make money."

These words were uttered as though straight from the mouth of God. Well, let's address some issues. First, "no man remembers the words of a poor wise man." Is that so? What about John the Baptist who lived on locust and wild honey in the wilderness? Are his words forgotten? Jesus even questioned the multitude as to why they would go listen to poor John, in poor apparel, when they could listen to rich kings in palaces.

What about Elijah who lived in caves and deserts? Is it his words or Ahab's who stood the test of time? What about the disciples of Jerusalem who held all things in common so that none suffered want? Somehow I don't usually pair Bible prophets with country-club anointings. Jeremiah struggled constantly from the rejection of the wealthy and influential. Perhaps he needed that money-making anointing. I just don't see the Lord saying this.

And since when is an abundance of money the assurance of freedom from covetousness? My Bible tells me that the rich have no rest because they are always worried about how to get more, but the poor sleep soundly (Eccles. 5:12). Not only do I judge this word as not from the Lord, but I judge it as unscriptural. Yet, I could tell as I listened to the tape that the man giving the word was charged with emotion, and I heard the people in the background clapping and shouting. Yet I sensed no anointing or presence of God.

What effect did this word have on this young man? Did it strengthen him for hardship or battles? Did it draw his heart toward God? I questioned him, "How did you feel while this was being spoken over you? Did this make you feel good?"

He said, "Yes."

I asked, "Did the word make you want to embrace the prophet delivering the word?"

Again he said, "Yes."

Time had passed and I questioned further, "Do you believe this was a word from God?"

"No," he answered.

People go to this speaker's meetings hoping to receive a word from God. But really they want insight into their future. So is this minister a prophet or a Christian fortuneteller?

NO DINKY CHURCHES

A pastor relayed to me a word given to his son by another well-known prophet. The pastor said, "John, if you knew my son you would know this was about the worst possible word he could have been given. It fed a weakness in him, because my son sometimes

61

goes to the extreme of being overconfident."

The pastor then shared how the prophet told his son God had called him to full-time ministry. He went on and on about how powerful and great the ministry would be. He then said, "You'll never have to pastor some dinky little fifty-member church . . . "

How heartbreaking! Many "dinky little fifty-member churches" are precious to God and are in obedience to Him. There are some five-thousand-member churches that have wandered further from the heart and ways of God than many "dinky" ministries. Numbers are significant from the viewpoint of man, but God sees things differently. Yet again the word was given as though straight from the mouth of God.

To obey the word, the young man's parents spent a lot of money and time on Bible school, and now their son is pursuing a career in the secular market. This pastor confessed to me that he didn't believe his son was ever called to be in full-time ministry.

BABIES, BABIES, BABIES

A prophetic speaker came to a church of a well-known pastor and prophesied before the entire congregation that he and his wife were going to have another child. This really upset the pastor because he and his wife already had several and they had taken surgical measures to prevent pregnancy.

My wife was prophesied over after our third son that her next child would be a girl (though she has always wanted sons). When she became pregnant a year later she assumed it must be a girl. The day before her sonogram she prayed and asked God, "This is a girl, right?" God told her firmly, "No!" The next day the sonogram confirmed it was a baby boy. Yet Lisa was constantly plagued by people who had heard the word or had words of their own that the baby was a girl. She was stopped at almost every meeting and told it was a girl. One woman called with a dream that we thought it was a boy and then it was a girl. Another said she was praying that God would change the baby to a girl in the womb (which we immediately rebuked and bound). Lisa told them the sonogram showed a boy, and they responded, "Sonograms have been wrong before." To this, Lisa replied, "So have the prophetesses." The confrontations didn't stop until the birth of our fourth son, Arden.

The most tragic baby prophecy I know of was one where a minister called out a young, unmarried virgin and told her that the Lord had showed him she was pregnant. This girl was visiting friends at this church and was engaged. This humiliated her in front of the whole assembly. She argued that it wasn't possible, and he argued back that the Lord had shown him it was true. When confronted after the service, he backed down and changed his word to say that when she got married she would have a little girl. She is presently married and has been for a few years now. There was never a child out of wedlock. As far as the little girl, well, there is a fifty-fifty chance on that one.

WEDDING BELLS

A woman my wife knows was told by two different well-respected "prophets" and a pastor that she was to marry the man she had just started dating. The prophecies spoke of the babies they would have together, and how long it would be before they were married. The prophecies told of God's marvelous plans for them.

The only problem was this man was filled with lust, would swear when frustrated, and was a moocher. He couldn't hold a job, and she ended up supporting him financially in various areas. All the signs told her to end the relationship, but she didn't want to go against the word that had been given. If she left him she would be leaving a God-ordained relationship.

After a two-year nightmare she finally cut it off. She was devastated. Three years later, I asked her if she believed it was God's will for them to be married. Her response was, "Absolutely not." Thank God they didn't marry.

TRAINED BY HARVARD

One man in his forties that my family and I know and love is a gifted craftsman and handyman. He loves serving ministries and has helped us as well as many others. A couple of years ago he was told by a well-respected prophetic minister that he would astound men of the world with his business knowledge and wisdom. To this he would answer that he had learned it from his schooling at Harvard. After receiving this word, our friend called wanting to know how he could enroll in Harvard through correspondence. I was taken back by his request because I knew he had a rough time graduating from high school, but he had a good job working in maintenance.

Shortly thereafter I stopped hearing from this friend. I called another minister recently and found out he is working two jobs to make ends meet—one as a bellman and the other as a clerk in a department store. The word pulled him off course and threw him into the pursuit of its fulfillment.

A PAY-BACK WORD

Many years ago when my wife and I first traveled we faced several disappointments with a couple of ministers. There were things said about us that were not true, which created an atmosphere of intense testing for us.

My wife attended a meeting of a well-known prophetic minister who is considered to be very accurate. In the meeting Lisa was called out and asked to stand. The minister acknowledged knowing little about us or what we had been through and then proceeded to give a word to my wife. The word was real encouraging and made us look and feel good. It identified us as being in the ministry and then came out with words similar to this, "The Lord says, 'They have spoken against you in private, but I am going to make them apologize publicly!'" My wife was in tears. *God has identified my hurt and pain and comforted me in it,* she thought. She left the meeting making a mental list of those who owed her an apology and thinking, *OK, now I know everybody who is against me, but God is on my side.*

When she came home and played the tape of her personal word I listened and then said, "Lisa, this is not from God. Jesus said, 'Father, forgive them, for they do not know what they do' (Luke 23:34). Not, 'Father make them apologize publicly.' All this word is doing is diverting our focus back to us and our past pain. We've

forgiven and released these people. I'm not looking for an apology."
She agreed. To date, no one has apologized privately, let alone publicly.

The danger of our embracing this word—even though it was accurate about our past—is that it would have aborted a work of character in our lives and diverted our future course.

THE FALSE ACCEPTED AS REAL

Hundred of thousands of these types of words have been released into the church in the last few years at all levels—personal, local, church, conference, and nationally. I've used examples of prophetic words given by respected prophets or ministries for this reason: to illustrate how this is so easily embraced nationwide. I have also not chosen the extremely obviously wrong words but tried to portray a sampling of typical personal words we hear frequently in the church.

I believe as you examine closely the form and function of prophetic utterances in the Scripture references I laid out at the beginning of this chapter and compare them to what we have today, it will help restore a proper standard for discerning and judging of prophecy.

We can become accustomed to the lie for so long that we no longer have a stomach for the truth. Soon we think the abnormal is normal. If the early church leaders from the Book of Acts attended some of our prophetic conferences their mouths would drop open in utter shock and amazement. They would then weep as Jeremiah, hearts broken by the pollution of the prophetic ministry.

What has happened? Why has the church not only tolerated but embraced the perversion of this ministry? The next chapter reveals the sobering truth. It will explain why our eyes have been blind and how we lost our discernment of the true from the false.

Contentment and covetousness are opposing forces. Contentment moves us away from idolatry and closer to the heart of God while covetousness distances us from God and drives us to the altars of idolatry.

7

SPEAKING TO THE IDOLS
OF THE HEART

Why are so many misled through these "prophetic" words? Why do we so often fail to discern between the true and false? In the last chapter we learned one reason for this: We have not used true biblical prophecy as a frame of reference.

The second reason is subtler. It is not born out of a failure to comprehend scriptural patterns. It is rooted in secret. We embrace these words because they feed the secret desires and motivations of our hearts. They have fed the soulish desire for gain and promotion. Without realizing it we have adopted a desire for the Pharisee's reward—the praise or recognition of man and the riches and comforts of this life. We have lost sight of the eternal reward and accepted the temporal. This inhibits our ability to rightly divide truth from falsehood.

To correctly explain this I must first define two words. Please pay close attention as you consider these definitions. Let your mind think just how they apply. Even though these words are familiar, let the Holy Spirit implant their meanings deep into your spirit.

COVETOUSNESS

The first one is *covetousness*. Let's look first at the root word *covet*. One of Webster's definitions is "to desire or wish for, with eagerness;

to desire earnestly to obtain or possess."

Webster's further defines the word *covetousness* as "a strong desire of obtaining and possessing some supposed good."

In prayer I asked the Lord for His definition of covetousness. His response was, "Covetousness is the desire for gain."

This does not limit covetousness to the desire for money. This encompasses possessions, position, comfort, acceptance, pleasure, power, lust, and so on. Covetousness is the state we find ourselves in when we're not content. We strive because we lack peace or rest with what God has given us. We resist His plan or process in our life.

Covetousness is the very opposite of contentment. The Bible tells us that "godliness with contentment is great gain" (1 Tim. 6:6). Godly contentment holds within itself great gain and a peace that transcends understanding. In contrast, covetousness is a dwelling of unrest and is fueled by ceaseless desires and lust. It is a state where both the deceptive and destructive are eminent.

Some may ask, "But didn't Paul himself tell us to 'covet earnestly the best gifts'?" (1 Cor. 12:31, KJV). Yes, but his instruction should be taken in context. He told us to intently desire the best gifts for the purpose of edifying or building up the church (1 Cor. 14:12). That means the motive behind this desire is to see others benefit through the plan and purpose of God. When our desires are pure, we don't care whether it is us or another used to disperse His gifts. We just want to be sure God's people are receiving from Him. If we have been entrusted with gifts, we cannot be concerned with the reactions of man. We must strive for the acceptance of God. Only then will we be faithful to speak what men need, not what they want. We'll be kingdom minded.

If we possess the desire of God's heart it won't matter who brings in the harvest—just that the harvest is brought in! Too often we lack His motive and yield to the power of covetousness even when it comes to God's power and anointing. We'll travel a hundred miles for a double-portion service or to get a word, yet we will not confront the envy and selfish motives hidden in our heart. It is easier to pursue the power while neglecting to pursue His purity and holiness.

While on vacation with my family we found a Christian channel and watched as a popular television evangelist taught a huge crowd on the anointing. He shared the price of it as the people listened intently. It was not hard to detect their passion for the power of God. Some even stood and stared at him with fire in their eyes. However, I sensed a grieving in my spirit. This was confirmed as I watched a man walk up and place a check in the hands of the evangelist. It was an offering. My mind flashed back to Peter, when he was offered a financial gift for the anointing (Acts 8:18–24). I watched with relief as this evangelist returned the check to the man.

I went outside and walked alone on the beach. "Lord," I questioned, "I sensed a grieving. . . . I think I know why, but I want You to explain it to me."

I heard His still small voice speak in my heart. "John, they're passionate for My power but for the wrong reasons. Power can make a person feel significant. It gives them authority, validates them, or brings them wealth."

Then I remembered Jesus' words to the multitude on judgment day. They professed His lordship, evidenced by the fact that they had done miracles, cast out demons, and prophesied in His name. He turns to them and says, "Depart from Me, you who did not do the will of My Father!" (Matt. 7:21–23, paraphrased).

The Lord continued, "John, notice the people didn't say, 'Lord, Lord, we visited those in prison in Your name, and we fed the hungry and clothed the naked in Your name.'"

Sobered, I agreed, "No, they didn't."

I then saw how so many covet His gifts for selfish or self-serving reasons, not out of love for Jesus and His people. This is but one way covetousness has crept into the church. We've allowed, and in some cases even encouraged, an inordinate desire for power or ministry.

CONTENTMENT

We've already mentioned this word. Now we'll define it. Webster's defines *content* or *contentment* as "rest or quietness of the mind in the present condition; satisfaction which holds the mind in peace, restraining complaint, opposition, or further desire, and often implying a moderate degree of happiness."

In prayer I asked the Lord for His simple definition of contentment. In my heart I heard, "Complete satisfaction in My will."

Jesus' life is the very picture of contentment. We hear this repeatedly in His words, "My food is to do the will of Him who sent Me, and to finish His work" (John 4:34). His perfect contentment with and commitment to God's will is evident in the messianic psalm, which reads: "I delight to do Your will, O my God, and Your law is within my heart" (Ps. 40:8).

No desire or passion existed for Him outside the will of God. His only passion was to fulfill the desires of His Father. From this contentment was born the words: "I live because of the Father" (John 6:57). This produced unearthly security and stability, so much so He boldly proclaimed, "I know where I came from and where I am going" (John 6:57; 8:14). Because of this He could not be deterred or misled!

Jesus lived solely for the Father's desire, and His complete and confident satisfaction was found in the performance of the Father's will. We are exhorted:

> Let your conduct [behavior] be without covetousness; be content with such things as you have. For He Himself has said, "I will never leave you nor forsake you."
>
> —HEBREWS 13:5

Contentment with His will is freedom from covetousness. It is to be free from servitude to the taskmaster of self. This is the true rest in which every believer is to abide. We are told, "For he who has entered His rest has himself also ceased from his works" (Heb. 4:10). This place of rest provides great strength and confidence.

> For thus says the Lord GOD, the Holy One of Israel: "In returning and rest you shall be saved; in quietness and confidence shall be your strength."
>
> —ISAIAH 30:15

Scripture describes us as sheep who have wandered and strayed.

Yet salvation is not found merely in returning but in the combination of returning and *resting*. This Hebrew word for *saved* is *yasha*. Essentially this word means "to remove or seek to remove someone from a burden, oppression, or danger."[1]

One of Strong's definitions of it is "to be safe." In this state of rest or contentment we find safety from deception! Here we are not misled or led astray.

Prior to his conversion to Christianity Paul passionately pursued power, influence, and notoriety. His own words describe how Jesus transformed his life and ministry:

> I have learned how to be content (satisfied to the point where
> I am not disturbed or disquieted) in whatever state I am.
> —PHILIPPIANS 4:11, AMP

He learned to live in a place of divine rest. The Western church has so desperately lacked this contentment. Our present culture and society encourages a state of constant discontentment. It drives its inhabitants to strive and achieve more and more. We are trained in discontentment. We are perpetually assaulted by family, peers, advertising, media, and other avenues that tell us what we lack to achieve this world's fulfillment. If yielded to, this pressure will produce lofty ambitions and selfish, competitive goals.

Sadly, too often ministry goals follow this pattern. Dreams or callings are perverted to focus more on fulfilling, self-serving motives. Though the call may be genuine, the motives become adulterated or polluted. These ambitions are cleverly disguised with Christian or ministry dialogue, making them difficult to detect. No matter how it is disguised, it is still nothing less than covetousness!

IDOLATRY TODAY

Contentment and covetousness are opposing forces. *Contentment* moves us away from idolatry and closer to the heart of God while *covetousness* distances us from God and drives us to the altars of idolatry. Contrasting words with opposite meanings further illustrates their distinctions. By defining both of these words we gain a clearer picture of covetousness. It becomes easier to see how it has crept into the church under the guise of ministry or blessings to mask its true identity.

In light of this understanding let's examine the word *covetousness* through the words of God's prophet Ezekiel.

> And the word of the LORD came to me, saying, "Son of man, these men have set up their idols in their hearts, and put before them that which causes them to stumble into iniquity. Should I let Myself be inquired of at all by them?"
> —EZEKIEL 14:2–3

God lamented that His covenant people came before Him for counsel, direction, or wisdom with idols hidden in their hearts. It is not clear whether they were fully aware of their doings. It appears the truth was shielded from their eyes. The idols from which they had sought fulfillment now caused them to stumble into iniquity. This Hebrew word for *iniquity* is *awon*. It signifies an offense, whether intentional or not, against God's law.[2]

Notice God did not say they had set up idols in their living rooms, yards, or even under their trees. This is because all idolatry begins in the heart. Before we go any further we must define idolatry.

Idolatry is somewhat of a foreign word to the American church. We tend to disregard God's warnings concerning it as having no modern or current application for us. We have no golden statues or altars. We have no carved images out of stone or wood. You would be hard pressed to find someone raised in our Western culture involved in such practices. We know the truths found in the Scriptures still speak to us today; therefore, idolatry must have a current application. Let's examine the Scriptures to form our definition. Only then will we recognize the astonishing level of our entanglement.

The very first of the Ten Commandments is "I am the LORD your God . . . You shall have no other gods before Me" (Exod. 20:2–3). The Hebrew word for *gods* is *elohiym*. This word appears almost 2,250 times in the Old Testament. In nearly two thousand of these references the word is used to identify the Lord God. An example of this is Deuteronomy 13:4, "You shall walk after the LORD [Jehovah] your God [*elohiym*] and fear Him, and keep His commandments and obey His voice; you shall serve Him and hold fast to Him." You can see in this scripture that the Lord's name is given (*Jehovah*) and then He is referred to as our *elohiym*. He is God, the absolute authority and ultimate source. When God says you shall have no other gods (*elohiym*) before Him, He is saying, "I am your source for everything. Nothing else shall take My place." Jesus worded it like this, "As the living Father sent Me, and I live because of the Father, so he who feeds on Me will live because of Me" (John 6:57). We feed on what sustains us. It becomes our source of life. This is why Jesus refers to Himself as the Bread of Life (John 6:48).

An idol becomes a source for us. This can happen in any area of our lives. An idol takes the place God deserves. It can serve as a source for happiness, comfort, peace, provision, and so forth. God says, "You shall not make idols for yourselves" (Lev. 26:1). We are the ones who make it an idol. An idol's power lies within our hearts. So it is not always made with stone, wood, or precious metal.

An idol is anything we put before God in our lives! It is what we love, like, trust, desire, or give our attention to more than the Lord. An idol is that from which you draw your strength or that to which you give your strength. A believer is drawn into idolatry when he allows his heart to be stirred with discontentment and looks for satisfaction outside of God. This could be a person, possession, or activity. Idolatry, therefore, is founded in covetousness. Paul confirms this:

> Therefore put to death your members which are on the earth: fornication, uncleanness, passion, evil desire, and covetousness, which is idolatry.
>
> —COLOSSIANS 3:5

Idolatry is defined through Scripture as covetousness or a heart seeking selfish gain. Again, I want to emphasize this is not limited to material things. It could be just about anything. For example, the desire for recognition could be an idol. Temporary joy and strength comes with the desired reputation or fame while discouragement accompanies any lack of it. Competition arises for the attention and affection of others. As a result, the opinions of others become increasingly important. Eventually the opinion of man outweighs the opinion of God.

Another example could be the desire for companionship. John tells us, "Our fellowship is with the Father and with His Son Jesus Christ" (1 John 1:3). We are encouraged to enter and abide in the companionship of the Holy Spirit (2 Cor. 13:14). Out of this pure fellowship God will raise up healthy relationships with others in the body. He knows better than us what is necessary and healthy in relationships. But some doubt His concern, timing, or selection and become anxious. Their contentment is disrupted, and they doubt His provision. They begin to long for and seek fellowship outside of His plan and will. This is how so many find themselves in relationships that eventually decay or corrupt their walk with God. This is often how wrong choices are made for marriage. The idol of companionship overshadows all proper reason, and they end up stumbling.

Idolatry originates in the heart. A person can easily fall into it while attending services and professing faith in Jesus Christ. In the Old Testament Judah would walk after other gods by committing idolatry on every hill and under every green tree (Jer. 3:6). Then they would come to the temple of the Lord and stand before Him and worship (Jer. 7:1–11). In fact, through Ezekiel, God exposed their hypocrisy by pointing out that the people sacrificed to idols and "on the same day they came into My sanctuary" (Ezek. 23:39). They still came to the temple, but their hearts belonged to idolatry.

IDOLATRY AND PROPHETIC WORDS

With this understanding of idolatry, let us read again what God spoke through the prophet Ezekiel:

> And the word of the LORD came to me, saying, "Son of man, these men have set up their idols in their hearts, and put before them that which causes them to stumble into iniquity.

Should I let Myself be inquired of at all by them?

"Therefore speak to them, and say to them, 'Thus says the Lord GOD: "Everyone of the house of Israel who sets up his idols in his heart, and puts before him what causes him to stumble into iniquity, and then comes to the prophet, I the LORD will answer him who comes, according to the multitude of his idols."'"

—EZEKIEL 14:2–4

Wow! When people come before a prophet with idolatry—the desire for personal gain—in their hearts and request counsel or seek a prophetic word, they may get one, but the word is not going to be God's will. The New American Standard Bible says, "I the LORD will be brought to give him an answer in the matter in view of the multitude of his idols." Now hear what God has to say about the prophet:

> . . . but if the prophet does give the man the answer he desires [thus allowing himself to be a party to the inquirer's sin of idolatry], I the Lord will see to it that the prophet is deceived in his answer.
>
> —EZEKIEL 14:9, AMP

For the last several months during prayer the Lord has dealt with me about the counterfeit prophetic ministry. I've cried out for answers to what is behind these words so loosely given in the church today. In answer the Spirit of God led me to this chapter in Ezekiel. It became clear as I read these passages. I discovered the root of any misuse was some type of covetousness. I found out how God described His people and prophets in the time period when the counterfeit flourished alongside the true prophetic in Israel.

> Because from the least of them even to the greatest of them, everyone is given to covetousness; and from the prophet even to the priest, everyone deals falsely.
>
> —JEREMIAH 6:13

I began to glimpse the deeper spiritual workings behind this grave error. I could see the discontentment of the men and women who come to these services. Out of this has arisen the desire for what they think they lack in life. (Most often these are not needs but are nothing more than wants or lusts). This idolatry opens them up to receive words that speak directly to those wants or lusts and strengthens these desires or idols. All that is necessary for them to hear what they want is that they find "ministers" who are lacking in the area of the fear of God. These will be concerned with their reputation, appearance, growth, and agendas. They can be bought or persuaded with the right reward, thus they will speak to them in light of their desires rather by the faithful light of the Word of God.

The story in 2 Chronicles 18 illustrates how idols of the heart can draw unto themselves prophetic confirmation. Jehoshaphat, king of Judah had allied himself with Ahab, king of Israel, through the marriage of their children. This was not a good move for Jehoshaphat because he feared the Lord while Ahab was an idolater. After some time Jehoshaphat went to Samaria to visit Ahab.

Ahab asked Jehoshaphat if he and Judah would go to war along-side Israel to attack Syria. Jehoshaphat replied, "Why, of course! You and I are brothers, and my troops are yours to command. We will certainly join you in battle." But then Jehoshaphat added, "But first let's find out what the LORD says" (vv. 3–4, NLT).

So the king of Israel summoned all the prophets of Israel, four hundred men. Notice these were not prophets of Baal or another false god but prophets of the Lord God. (See verse 10, which says they spoke in the name of Jehovah.) The king asked them if he should go to war or refrain.

The prophets all with one accord answered, "Go ahead, for God will give you a great victory!"

Yet Jehoshaphat was not comfortable with the answers from this large company of prophets. The fear of God in his life had kept his discernment somewhat intact. He asked, "Is there not still a prophet of the LORD here that we may inquire of Him?" He knew these were prophets of Israel and that they had spoken in the name of Jehovah, but still something was not right.

Ahab said, "There is still one man by whom we may inquire of

76

the LORD; but I hate him, because he never prophesies good concerning me, but always evil. He is Micaiah."

Jehoshaphat said to Ahab, "Let not the king say such things!" Ahab hated Micaiah because he never prophesied to him what he wanted to hear. Micaiah didn't want anything from Ahab. He feared God more than man. He knew God was his source and that he'd rather please God than a wicked king. This kept him pure and free from the flattery in which the others operated.

Ahab then sent for Micaiah. While they were waiting for the man of God, the other "prophets of Jehovah" continued to prophesy before the two kings. One of them named Zedekiah, a Hebrew of the tribe of Benjamin (1 Chron. 7:6–10), made horns of iron for himself, and he said, "Thus says the LORD [Jehovah]: 'With these you shall gore the Syrians until they are destroyed.'"

Then all the prophets prophesied so, saying, "Go up to Ramoth Gilead and prosper, for the LORD will deliver it into the king's hand."

These were terrific and specific words "from God." They were edifying, encouraging, and comforting. The same prophetic words issued forth from almost every prophet in Israel. Surely there is safety in the multitude of prophets . . . right? And what really was uplifting is the prophecies were confirmation! (This term is many times mentioned in our acceptance of prophetic words.) They confirmed the exact desires of Ahab's heart! Yes, that is right. They spoke directly to his desire for gain.

Now while the prophets prophesied, the messenger found Micaiah and spoke to him, saying, "Now listen, the words of the prophets with one accord encourage the king. Therefore please let your word be like the word of one of them, and speak encouragement."

I have heard advice like that myself before. "John, encourage the people. Preach positive messages. Build them up. Give them personal words from the Lord that will comfort them. End your services with an up tempo song. Let them leave feeling good." They act as if the mere messenger can tamper with the message of the King! How utterly irreverent!

Micaiah's blunt response was, "As the LORD lives, whatever my God says, that I will speak." O Father, send us prophets who will do the same in our day!

When Micaiah came before Ahab he was asked the same question already answered by the other prophets. Micaiah at first told him what he wanted to hear: "Go and prosper, and they shall be delivered into your hand!"

Ahab became upset with Micaiah for he thought he was mocking him. Yet Micaiah was only illustrating what God had revealed to him about what had transpired with all the other four hundred prophets.

For then Micaiah spoke the true prophetic word: "I saw all Israel scattered on the mountains, as sheep that have no shepherd. And the LORD said, 'These have no master. Let each return to his house in peace.'"

Ahab turned to Jehoshaphat and said, "Did I not tell you he would not prophesy good concerning me, but evil?"

Then Micaiah proceeded to tell Ahab what caused the other prophets to tell him to go forth to battle.

> Therefore hear the word of the LORD: I saw the LORD sitting on His throne, and all the host of heaven standing on His right hand and His left. And the LORD said, "Who will persuade Ahab king of Israel to go up, that he may fall at Ramoth Gilead?" So one spoke in this manner, and another spoke in that manner. Then a spirit came forward and stood before the LORD, and said, "I will persuade him." The LORD said to him, "In what way?" So he said, "I will go out and be a lying spirit in the mouth of all his prophets." And the LORD said, "You shall persuade him and also prevail; go out and do so."
>
> —2 CHRONICLES 18:18–21

Micaiah then said:

> Therefore look! The LORD has put a lying spirit in the mouth of these prophets of yours, and the LORD has declared disaster against you.
>
> —VERSE 22

God answered Ahab according to the deception and idolatry in

78

his heart. Ahab received the words he wanted to hear but refused the true words of God that would have brought protection and deliverance. Ahab went out to battle and thought he'd be protected because he disguised himself so the Syrians could not recognize him. You can hide from man, but you can never hide from God! He was struck by a wild arrow and died before the day ended.

What about today? The "prophets of the Lord" are prophesying all over the land. They say "Thus saith the Lord . . ." so freely, but is it by the Spirit of God, or are their words inspired by deceptive forces of idolatry? Are idols resident in both the prophets' and the people's hearts? We must remember well Paul's warning: "For Satan himself transforms himself into an angel of light" (2 Cor. 11:14).

Paul does not say that Satan *can* transform himself into an angel of light—but that he *does!* It is Satan's prime mode of operation. This means he or his cohorts can mimic prophetic words in the mind of the prophet—words that sound as though the Spirit of God is speaking. Especially since God stated, "I the Lord will see to it that the prophet is deceived in his answer" (Ezek. 14:9, AMP). Remember, God gave the lying spirit permission to influence the prophets of Israel.

As in the days of Jeremiah and Ezekiel there are a multitude of words. They seem to be the majority, voicing prosperity, happiness, and peace. Instead of calling men and women back to the heart of God with sound words, they draw them away with words that feed the idols in their hearts. Paul foresaw this:

> For the time is coming when [people] will not tolerate (endure) sound and wholesome instruction, but, having ears itching [for something pleasing and gratifying], they will gather to themselves one teacher after another to a considerable number, chosen to satisfy their own liking and to foster the errors they hold.
>
> —2 TIMOTHY 4:3, AMP

These teachers or prophets will speak to the people in such a way that their covetous, idolatrous hearts will be satisfied. We must ask God for prophets like Micaiah who will speak faithfully the word of the Lord whether it is welcomed or not!

"MINISTRY IN ONE HAND AND MONEY IN THE OTHER"

My wife and I know a woman, whom I'll call Susan for the sake of her privacy. She attended a "prophetic" meeting. Susan is single and in her thirties. She had a tremendous desire to be married and to be in ministry. Susan had made it known to some that she was very tight financially. In the meeting she was told to stand. The well-known prophet had no idea who she was, yet he gave her this word: "Thus saith the Lord, 'I am bringing your husband to you, and he will have ministry in one hand and money in the other! I am preparing you for him even now.'" Then the "prophet" told her it would all happen quickly and she would be married in three months. Of course, she was in awe and overwhelmed with joy about what "God had spoken to her." She wept, sure that God had heard her heart's cry.

She prepared herself for this soon-coming husband with ministry and money in his hands. She went out and bought a wedding dress, even though her finances were tight. She also turned down a good job offer, knowing that her mate would soon arrive. Three months passed and not only did the wedding bells not ring—she didn't meet or develop any relationships with a man. In fact, at the time of this writing it has been more than five years, and still she is single. She has floated from one career to another and from one church to another, watching and waiting.

The prophetic word spoke directly to an inordinate desire in her heart. Marriage, ministry, and finances—all her areas of discontentment—were promised fulfillment. The personal prophecy confirmed the desires of her heart and appeared amazingly accurate, but was it from the Lord? Or was it inspired by another source? Judging by the fruit, both the prophet and Susan were deceived, yet they both fully believed it to be the words of the Holy Spirit!

I could give example after example of this very thing. In fact, I don't believe I'd be far off to say that the majority of personal words or prophecies fall into this category. Discontented inquirers attend meetings where men-pleasing "prophets" are easily induced to tell them what is in their hearts. The outcome is evident; the words reflect the covetous desires of the inquirers and the motives of the prophet. Both are deceived into thinking it is really the Lord speaking.

"You Will Work for the Evangelist"

Back in the early to mid-eighties I served in the ministry of helps for a very large church in Texas. One of my responsibilities was to care for visiting ministers. There was one particular evangelist who came regularly to our church whom I loved. He is well known in Third World nations and has seen millions come into the kingdom during his forty years of ministry.

I was very drawn to him, and every time he came to our church we would have wonderful fellowship. He gave me his home phone number and would write back to me when I wrote him. Over a four-year time period he gave me two complete wardrobes of his clothes, since our sizes were identical.

I wanted to work for this man in a bad way. Working for him became my focus for ministry and life. I am embarrassed to say this, but I remember times in my prayer closet when I would prophesy to myself that I would leave where I was and serve under this man as Elisha served under Elijah. I would ramble on and on about how I would go farther and do more than what even he had done. Then I would "prophetically" predict a double portion of the anointing of miracles and salvation. I was even so bold as to write these prophecies down on paper. My wife would hear me and tell me she was grieved, but I reasoned she was just resistant to change.

After two years something really exciting happened. Within a couple of months two different people prophesied that I would go and work for this evangelist. They even called him by name! I was beside myself with joy.

I started preparing myself. I wrote to him and shared my desire to work for him and his wife. Time passed, and we continued to move in that direction. Then suddenly God made it overwhelmingly apparent that this was not His will for us. It never had been. This realization shook me to my very core. I was devastated. For nearly four years the entire focus of my emotions, ministry, ambitions, and thoughts had been to work for him. All those close to me knew this as well. I felt ashamed and humiliated.

For weeks I walked around numb, both spiritually and emotionally. I remember thinking, *How did this happen? What about the prophetic words that were spoken over me? How could I have been so wrong? How could those prophecies have been so wrong?* I remember telling a pastor on the staff, "I feel as if I could walk under your office door. Everyone must think I'm a flake." But what frightened me the most was this haunting question: How will I know in the future if I am hearing from God?

It was painful, and it took a few months, but God not only healed me . . . He also restored me. I discovered that ministry had become an idol to me, and working for that man was the focus of my idolatry. The healing came one morning while in prayer. I heard God say, "John, put the ministry on the altar."

I had already repented of my excessive and incorrect desires, and after years of stress and striving I was more than ready to lay it down. I lifted my hands to symbolize my surrender, and from the depths of my being I spoke, "Lord, I place it on the altar. I give it back to You. If Jesus comes and I am still driving the van for my church and serving my pastor, You will not say that I disobeyed You." I experienced the peace of God as it flooded my soul for the first time in two years.

I asked the Lord, "Why are You having me do this?"

The Lord answered, "Because I wanted to see if you are serving Me or the dream!" His statement opened my eyes.

I stayed in that peace, guarding it carefully. In a matter of months God promoted me in His service, and I became an associate pastor. Ministry was no longer an idol!

The full understanding of how this all transpired did not come until more than ten years later as the Lord spoke to me through Ezekiel 14. I saw how I had erected the idol of ministry and embraced the words that spoke to it. I had spoken out of the idolatry in my own heart, and the two individuals who gave me words had spoken in response to my idolatry. These were deceptive words that brought confusion to my life and to the lives of those close to me. Jeremiah 17:9 tells us the heart is deceptive above all things. I had let my heart lead me astray. I had twisted the Scriptures to fulfill my desires and called my words God's.

Some may ask, "Was a lying spirit speaking through you and the other individuals?" It very well could have been, but that is not what I want to focus on. I want to focus on the deception. I deceived myself through my discontentment and inordinate desires. I was far from abiding in His rest as I labored to appease my own covetous heart.

Desire for success is a major force behind false prophecy's acceptance in the church. Listen to what God spoke through Jeremiah:

> Yes, this is what the LORD Almighty, the God of Israel, says:
> "Do not let the prophets and diviners among you deceive you.
> Do not listen to the dreams *you encourage them to have.*"
> —JEREMIAH 29:8, NIV, EMPHASIS ADDED

We've encouraged the prophets and diviners to speak to us according to our discontentment and idolatry! We have a part in it and must repent of our discontent and covetous desires for gain!

There is hope. Though we have wandered astray and followed after words of idolatry, it is not too late to return to the path of life. God warns us because He longs to restore us. He will forgive! He cleansed and restored me. I repented before God and all those affected by my sin of using His name in vain and speaking falsely. He is no respecter of man. He will do the same for any who will humble themselves and repent.

If you have spoken counterfeit prophetic words or strayed unto the path of deception due to idolatry, you need to know His forgiveness is available through repentance. In this next chapter we will see the consequences of submitting to a counterfeit prophetic ministry or word.

False prophecy defiles people,
and this defilement makes
them barren and useless.

8

DEFILED BY PROPHETIC WORDS

I sat across the lunch table from a good friend at a restaurant where we had frequently eaten. At the time I didn't realize it would be our last lunch together at this familiar spot. This man and his wife were good friends of ours. We all worked together on staff at a large church in Texas. I admired them as a model Christian couple. They worked hard and were involved in multiple ministry outreaches. He was a prayer warrior and headed up the intercessory prayer support for the outreaches. Each time I saw him, there was always a kind word of encouragement. I never saw him as selfish; he was always genuine in his concern for others no matter who they were. He was humble and teachable and endeavored to walk in holiness. At that time if you'd asked me, "Who is the most on-fire believer you know?," without hesitation my answer would have been him.

Suddenly he announced his resignation from the church staff. He had come to my office with his usual smile and shared how he had been asked to join the sales team of a very good company. The growth potential was excellent. I was confused. Though the offer sounded good, I couldn't shake the thought that this man should be in ministry. It was where his heart was. At the time I said nothing and figured he knew what he was doing.

A few months after his departure we heard the terrible news. It spread through the church staff like wildfire. He and his wife were divorced. How could this be! They appeared so strong in their walk with God and in their relationship with each other. But as it turned out they were very good at covering their deep marriage problems. No one identified the hidden mounting tension between them. Even their best friends were shocked. Their divorce was finalized quickly and quietly.

Across the table from him now I repeated the question that had plagued me since I'd heard the news.

"How did this all happen?" I asked pointedly.

He held my gaze with firm but sad eyes. "John, when my wife and I were dating, our former pastor called us out in a service and prophesied that God had called us to be married. I was a young believer and loved God with all my heart. I didn't want to disappoint Him, so I married her even though I didn't love her. The entire time we were married I pleaded with God, asking Him to give me the love for her a man should have for his wife. That love never came, and it became increasingly difficult until I couldn't bear it. I know I've sinned by divorcing her, but I felt hopeless."

My heart sank and my appetite left. I was newly married and a young believer as well. This was my first encounter with a counterfeit word. I looked at my devastated friend. The sparkle in his eyes was gone. His countenance was heavy and solemn. It was as though I could see a root of bitterness settling in. I reached out to him as best as I could and assured him that I wouldn't reject him.

The fact he worked for a secular sales company and had stopped attending the church made contact with him difficult. An opportunity opened up for him in another state, and he was gone only a few short months after our lunch.

Later I found out how to reach him and called him. He shared how he attended a traditional church and was in no way involved in ministry. He no longer wanted anything to do with what he called "demonstrative Christianity."

Through his measured tones I heard a cold numbness. It was evident his fire was gone and that he'd only told me where he stood to keep me from probing any deeper. He was shipwrecked and his passion was gone.

Made Worthless

There is another factor in this tragic tale: It is quite possible that to this day the pastor who gave them the "thus saith the Lord" to be married is totally unaware of the damage it wreaked in the life of this young couple. More than likely he continues to give what seems to be exciting and harmless prophetic words to individuals. But this is not limited to him. There are numerous others who utter these unbridled words to individuals, whether it is in a private setting, church, seminar, or prophetic conference. There is a severe lack of accountability. Most do not realize they are corrupting and destroying lives through presumption. It is a tragedy that must be confronted. We must heed the warning of the Lord:

> Thus says the LORD of hosts: "Do not listen to the words of the prophets who prophesy to you. They make you worthless; they speak a vision of their own heart, not from the mouth of the LORD."
>
> —JEREMIAH 23:16

God warns that these words can be spoken from the prophet's heart, not by the mouth of the Lord. When this happens, the spoken word has the power to cause its hearer to become worthless. We must not forget that words have power to heal or to destroy (Prov. 18:21). *God's Word* has the power to transform us to fulfill His purpose, while *man's word* has the power to destroy this purpose. This Hebrew word for *worthless* is *habal*. It is a root word that means "to be vain in act, word, or expectation." The New American Standard reads, "They are leading you into futility" (Jer. 23:16, NAS). Other words that describe this Hebrew word are "useless" or "fruitless."

God describes how the counterfeit prophecy makes a person useless by saying that from these prophets, "pollution has gone forth into all the land" (Jer. 23:15, NAS). To *pollute* something is to defile it (Webster's dictionary). It is to take something that once was pure and mix into it the impure. False prophecy defiles people, and this defilement makes them barren and useless!

87

Unfortunately, once someone has been defiled by such words they become blinded to their destructiveness until much later. This is usually after the damage has been done.

A YOUNG MINISTER DEFILED

There is a precious family we know that has been in full-time ministry for four generations. The elder of their two sons had just recently married a godly young lady. He was very involved with his parent's ministry and is extremely gifted himself in ministry and music. The hand of God is very evident on his life to continue the heritage of ministry in which his family has walked.

He and his wife went to a well-known prophetess's meeting. He was given a word that he would operate in great technical wisdom. The prophetess said his engineering skills would bring forth bridges and buildings. This man did have a keen mind when it came to music, but he was weak in math. He had no training whatsoever in any type of construction or engineering.

He knew I had studied engineering and worked as one for a short while, so he called to talk about it. He told my wife, Lisa, about the word and also shared his apprehension that he was weak in science and math and asked her advice. He was planning on enrolling in a junior college to take some courses. Lisa did not bear witness with any of it. She warned him that he was seeking to fulfill a word instead of seeking God. She voiced her concern. He responded that he was discontented at the recording studio and thought it might be exciting to go another direction.

So he left the ministry and enrolled in school to study engineering. When my wife and I heard what he had done, we were concerned but determined to stay out of it, not wanting to interfere.

Months went by, and we learned this young couple was struggling financially. Out of concern I called and learned that if they did not come up with their rent money in two days they would be evicted. They had already moved once trying to save money. I was outraged. I confronted him about this prophecy he had received about becoming an engineer, which was something I probably should have done sooner.

I got very strong with him. He was confused and hesitant. I felt as though I wasn't talking to the same young man I'd known a year earlier. He'd always been so bright and focused. Now it was as if he were in a cloud. He was unsure and confused. Confusion is often the product of false words.

He alluded to the fact he was in a transition and looking for direction when he got this prophetic word. Before he received the word, I could see his passion for involvement with his parent's ministry had lessened. He loved his parents and respected their ministry, but the truth was God was weaning him in preparation for the next step in his life. I am convinced this prophetess discerned the restlessness in his soul and spoke an appealing "thus saith the Lord." Of course, this was not God's oracle, just one that offered him a fresh start. Nevertheless, it was not God's fresh start!

I told him, having been an engineer, that I honestly could not see him as one. I told him that when I'd heard he'd received this word a few months earlier I was grieved. I also explained that if God was in it there would be provision for he and his wife. He softened, and I sensed he was about to emotionally break down under the pressure.

I said, "Let's pray together, bind confusion, and ask for God's will."

He agreed.

I remember that as we prayed over the phone a powerful presence of God filled both my office and his apartment. I felt my voice rise, strengthened by the power of God. Then I heard the Holy Spirit say, "Break divination off of his life." I was taken back by this, because the prophetic minister who spoke over him was well respected. I obeyed and broke divination off him. As I did the power and presence of God increased. I heard him crying on the other end of my phone.

When I was finished, he was weeping, and his wife was rejoicing in the background. The next day money was given to them for their rent, and before the week was out his wife was hired in a good position in a local company. He found a job as well. A few short months later he was offered an associate pastor position at a wonderful church in California. This was where God wanted them, and it is where they are even now.

This couple had been defiled by divination through a word spoken in the name of the Lord. You say, *Divination?* Yes, that's right. *Divination* is the imitation of the divine.

Through Ezekiel, God said of the prophets of Israel:

> They have envisioned futility and false divination, saying, "Thus says the LORD!" But the LORD has not sent them; yet they hope that the word may be confirmed.
> —EZEKIEL 13:6

The Hebrew word for *divination* is *qecem.* It means "an oracle," yet it is not from the Lord. Simply put, these prophets speak their own oracles as though they were God's. Yet the words are not God's but their own. This is another way of describing the imitation or counterfeit of the true prophetic word of the Lord.

The divination defiled this couple and reduced them to a state of limbo or barren uselessness. Again, remember God's warning: "Do not listen to the words of the prophets who prophesy to you. They make you worthless; they speak a vision of their own heart, not from the mouth of the LORD" (Jer. 23:16).

MY WIFE'S EXPERIENCE

My wife and I first became keenly aware of this defilement when we received a word from a well-respected prophet. Lisa and I were new on staff at a large ministry. This minister was brought in to minister to the staff in the fellowship hall. We were seated in a circle while he went before each staff member and gave each a personal word.

I believe practices like prophesying to everyone in a small group is presumptive. We are to prophesy as the Spirit of God wills, not as we will it. We do not dictate who receives messages, rather He dictates it to us. The method seems very mechanical and not Spirit led.

When he came to us he spoke elaborate words about me, all about where I'd left and where I was going. But he said almost nothing to my wife. It was as if she did not exist. After he was through I was excited. I looked at Lisa and could tell she was feeling uncomfortable. We are very much a team, and I wondered if she felt left out. I pulled him aside after the meeting and asked him to prophesy to Lisa alone this time.

He pulled us out of the room and sat us down. He looked at my wife and asked her where she was from. She replied, "I'm from where he is from," pointing to me.

He then proceeded to say "what the Lord was saying about her." He described her as a person who didn't handle stress very well and that she had just come out of one of the roughest times of her life. He assured her God was now going to hide her in the secret place of His presence, free from the strife of tongues. He explained, "You'll be a barometer for your husband, and whenever you can't handle the stress any longer it will be a signal for John to draw back."

As Lisa and I walked out of the building, I apologized to her. "I guess I shouldn't have asked for the second one. That wasn't God."

But Lisa was disturbed. Not only did she handle stress well—she thrived under it. She looked perplexed and said, "If that word is true, then I'm going to take up knitting. I'm not going to be some basket case who holds you back by whining so that you have to come home and baby me." Then she hesitated and questioned me, "Do you think I freak under pressure?"

I reassured her, "Honey, that wasn't God. Don't worry about it."

There were other errors in the word. The last year of our marriage had been wonderful. We were so close and very much one in purpose. Lisa was active with the girls of our youth group and a great support and encouragement to me. Things had never been so good! Yet he said she was coming out of an extremely rough time.

The next day Lisa found out she was pregnant with our second child. She thought, *Well, maybe this man was right. Maybe God is going to use me for breeding purposes and just put me out to pasture.*

The next nine months of our life ended up being the toughest months we had ever faced. Persecution and attacks seemed to arise from every source. The stress of those months was almost unbearable. Lisa withdrew into a depression. A cloud had come over her that she could not shake. The words of the prophecy haunted her memory. She now was buckling under the type of pressure upon which she had previously thrived. I lost the strength of her support at my side as she tried to dodge the darts.

Right before Austin was born, a man of God came to our church. His preaching was bold and brought strength and encouragement. Though he never said one "thus saith the Lord," his words were life giving and carried powerful and liberating truths. As Lisa listened, these words penetrated deeper than the previous lie. The light of God's Word pierced through the veil of darkness.

One evening shortly after this service she came to me. "John, I've been under a cloud of depression ever since I was given that word. Even though I didn't believe it, I have lived under the constant fear and dread of it. John, as my husband you need to break these words off my life. I feel a curse was released, and you need to replace it with God's truth and blessing."

We joined hands as we sat on our bed together and prayed until we sensed the leading of the Holy Spirit. Together we broke the power of that word and the depression, fear, and oppression that had accompanied it. God's Word says:

> "No weapon formed against you shall prosper, and every tongue which rises against you in judgment you shall condemn. This is the heritage of the servants of the LORD, and their righteousness is from Me," says the LORD.
> —ISAIAH 54:17

Notice God says "you shall condemn" the words spoken against you. When words of false divination are spoken they carry with them a spiritual force. That force will continue to attack us until we break the words. Once the words are broken then the power behind them is broken. This will be discussed in greater depth in chapter fifteen.

That prophecy was divination, which rendered Lisa ineffective as my wife and helpmeet. It brought torment and confusion, and the words displaced her from my side for nine months. Had God not sent someone to speak His true prophetic word, there is no way of knowing how long the oppression would have lasted. God said, "Do not listen to the words of the prophets who prophesy to you. They make you worthless; they speak a vision of their own heart, not from the mouth of the LORD" (Jer. 23:16).

ALL THREE CHILDREN AFFECTED

I know a pastor who has three children, and each of them has suffered extended periods of barrenness due to such words. Both he and his wife are godly, and they have a growing church. Lisa shared the subject matter of this book with them when she was there. They were very supportive and told what had happened in the lives of their children. They had invited a few nationally well-known prophetic ministries to their church and were still suffering the consequences. I called them later to hear the accounts firsthand from both the husband and wife.

A different prophetic person affected each child. The couple has two sons and one daughter. The oldest son was given a word that he would have a powerful ministry. God would take him straight to the top, and he would be a great pastor. When the time came for him to go on to higher education, he went to Bible school. It seemed the only thing for him to do in light of the word he'd received. He spent aimless months there because he lacked the inward passion that comes with a true call from God. A lot of time and money was spent. Finally the son admitted to his parents that he didn't even feel called to the ministry.

When he received the word, he didn't say anything because he didn't want to disappoint God or his father. He felt compelled to pursue it. The father admitted he did not sense a calling on his son, but he too was reluctant to speak against "the word of the Lord."

His mother told me, "My son to this day fights guilt because he doesn't feel called to be a pastor of any church." The son is now pursuing a job in the secular arena. Though this word was uttered in moments, it set this young man on a barren path of discouragement. Those years were wasted, and only now is he pursuing what he probably should have in the first place. Yet a false guilt still trails him.

FLYING FOR JESUS

Their other son was told he would fly airplanes for the Lord. God would use him to transport ministers, missionaries, ministry supplies, and so on. When he was old enough to work, he saved his money for a number of years to finance flying lessons. He spent all he made doing so. There was a problem though. He became terribly airsick each time he flew. He was terrified of flying but wanted to be obedient. In desperation he finally came to his father and shared his extreme dislike for flying, and asked if he would be in disobedience to stop. His father supported him and told him he thought it would be all right to quit the lessons, but the son couldn't shake the pressure from the word, so he continued.

Later during his solo training he cried out to God in the plane, "Lord, I hate flying." In his heart he heard God answer, "It's okay; I never told you to do it." This immediately relieved him of the pressure to fulfill the false word. It took a true word to break the power of a false one. That was his last flight.

This defilement lasted five years. Again, words spoken in moments had led him down a path of discouragement and disappointment. Financially he'd saved for years to finance the flight lessons, so this money was lost for any other form of education. He'd suffered physical and mental exhaustion while trying to do something he hated. On top of this, he fought guilt for his fear of flying.

I believe the worst repercussion of the counterfeit prophetic was what happened to their daughter. Her story is an example of a heart condition that results when words are spoken in support of the areas God wants crucified in the church. We will discuss this one in detail in the next chapter.

It takes spiritual fortitude to reject what would bring happiness in order to embrace what is difficult.

9

TAUGHT MY PEOPLE REBELLION

In the previous chapter we learned false prophecies can pollute or defile people's lives. The level of this defilement may vary. I know some who have suffered physical affliction from divination. A fog of confusion and depression has shrouded the emotions of others. But the following consequence is what I consider the most detrimental or dangerous. It is exemplified with what happened to the daughter of this pastor.

"MONEY WILL BE PUT IN YOUR HANDS"

Their daughter was away at college, and she was in the midst of a very rough semester. A well-known prophetess gave her the following word: "Don't get a summer job; don't work; God will see to it that people will just hand you money." She was also told God wanted her to "stay on a continual high" and that she was not to listen to anyone who told her to live a balanced Christian life.

In her mother's words, "This caused much confusion since she fights depression and is rarely on a 'continual high.'" The word caused a conflict for her parents. Their scriptural work ethic did not agree with a life without work. But now their daughter was armed with her word. Though she had formerly been submissive to her parents, now she changed. In her mother's words, she "really rebelled against us as parents all summer, refusing to work. She ended up broke because no one handed her money—especially us."

This word had made this young lady feel special and elite. It fed an area of pride in her life. God favored her so much that He didn't want her to work but just to enjoy herself while others worked to support her. But the summer passed and the origin or root of the word was revealed. The word was not from God. Scripture tells us the tongue "can ruin your whole life. It can turn the entire course of your life into a blazing flame of destruction, for it is set on fire by hell itself" (James 3:6, NLT).

When we agree with and receive words that appeal to us but are not from God, we open our lives to deception and ruin. James said these words are set on fire by hell itself. This is why God sternly warns, "Do not listen to the words of the prophets who prophesy to you. They make you worthless; they speak a vision of their own heart, not from the mouth of the LORD" (Jer. 23:16)!

These counterfeit prophetic words undermined years of godly parental teaching and training. Rebellion was encouraged with ethics that were unscriptural. Not to mention that a bad example was set before the entire church and the friends of this pastor's daughter.

Some of you may at this time be questioning, "What about young prophets, the ones who are just developing their gifts? Maybe they just missed it?" In answer we must remember that true prophets do not speak of their own accord, but they speak as the Holy Spirit comes upon them. The Holy Spirit is not in training, and He only speaks the true and the pure. The error comes when we speak when He has not or we are silent when He is speaking. Even Saul in all his torment gave true prophetic words when he was overshadowed by the Holy Spirit (1 Sam. 19:24). Samuel, when he was only a boy, gave a pure and fully accurate prophecy his first time (1 Sam. 3:11–19). He did not have to "grow in the gift."

FALSE PROPHECY FOSTERS REBELLION

Most often prophetic defilement brings forth rebellion. A good illustration of this is found in the Book of Jeremiah. Judah had become a nation of covetous people. They no longer heeded God's statutes and judgments. They had turned from following the living God and departed the path of their faithful fathers. They sought the comfort and pleasures this world offers. All the while they believed they were in right standing with the Lord, yet they lived according to the dictates of their own heart. They then stood before Him at the temple and proclaimed, "'We are safe!' [Amplified says, "We are set free!"]—only to go right back to all those evils again" (Jer. 7:10, NLT).

God warned them repeatedly through prophets, but their voices were small amid the majority who proclaimed prosperity and peace to a covetous people. Jeremiah was one of the final voices of warning before God's judgment overtook them. But they would not listen because the idolatry in their hearts had been strengthened by the words of divination and flattery. Their ways became set and their hearts hardened by the numerous prophets of ease and peace. Judgment was eminent.

The first wave of judgment came when the king of Babylon, Nebuchadnezzar, took Judah's king captive and set up another to rule in his place. He carried the king and many others off to Babylon along with valuable articles from the house of the Lord. Even this did not get their full attention.

A few years passed and in obedience to the word of the Lord, Jeremiah took a wooden yoke upon himself, symbolizing the extent of Israel's judgment under Nebuchadnezzar. Jeremiah spoke this word of the Lord to the king of Judah and the people, "Bow your neck under the yoke of the king of Babylon; serve him and his people, and you will live" (Jer. 27:12, NIV). This certainly was not what they wanted to hear, but soon they had the word they wanted to hear. It came through Hananiah, a prophet from Gibeon. He spoke against Jeremiah's earlier prophecies in the temple in the presence of the priests and all the people. He said, "Thus speaks the LORD of hosts, the God of Israel, saying: 'I have broken the yoke of the king of Babylon. Within two full years I will bring back to this place all the vessels of the LORD's house, that Nebuchadnezzar king of Babylon took away from this place and carried to Babylon. And I will bring back to this place Jeconiah the son of Jehoiakim, king of Judah, with all the captives of Judah who went to Babylon,' says the LORD, 'for I will break the yoke of the king of Babylon'" (Jer. 28:2–4).

I am sure this prophetic word was well received by the people. It brought edification and comfort. It promised the blessings of restoration. It spoke kindly to those who had suffered loss and assured the fulfillment of God's promises. Most likely the people were praising God and some even weeping for joy.

Only Jeremiah's response was different. Instead of rejoicing, he confronted the prophet. "From early times the prophets who preceded you and me have prophesied war, disaster and plague against many countries and great kingdoms. But the prophet who prophesies peace will be recognized as one truly sent by the LORD only if his prediction comes true" (Jer. 28:8–9, NIV). The New Living Translation says:

> So a prophet who predicts peace must carry the burden of proof. Only when his predictions come true can it be known that he is really from the LORD.
> —JEREMIAH 28:9, NLT

Prophets who prophesy peace and prosperity are recognized as true only if their predictions come true. If implemented, this standard would eliminate many questions today! Why wasn't the standard the same for prophets who prophesied war, disaster, and plague? The reason is if there was repentance the disaster was often averted or postponed. We see this with Nineveh when Jonah warned of pending judgment in forty days. They repented, and the judgment was averted. This did not make Jonah a false prophet. It revealed God as merciful.

After Hananiah the prophet heard Jeremiah's words, he boldly took the yoke from off Jeremiah's neck and broke it before the people. Then Hananiah declared, "Thus says the LORD: 'Even so I will break the yoke of Nebuchadnezzar king of Babylon from the neck of all nations within the space of two full years'" (v. 11). After this display, Jeremiah left the temple.

Then the word of the Lord came to Jeremiah, saying, "Go and

tell Hananiah, saying, 'Thus says the LORD: "You have broken the yokes of wood, but you have made in their place yokes of iron"'" (Jer. 28:12–13). He continued to tell by the word of the Lord how the Lord had given dominion to Nebuchadnezzar. Jeremiah then said to Hananiah the prophet:

> This year you shall die, because you have taught rebellion against the LORD.
>
> —JEREMIAH 28:16

How did Hananiah's words of restoration and peace teach rebellion? God had told the people to submit to Nebuchadnezzar. He told them to build houses and plan to stay. He told them to plant gardens, marry, and have children and grandchildren. He told them to multiply and not to dwindle. He told them to pray for the peace and prosperity of their captors and then they would enjoy peace also (Jer. 29:4–7). You live one way if you are only staying in a city for two years and quite another if you know you'll be there for seventy. The word Hananiah gave would cause them to behave the opposite of how God wanted them to.

Too often we limit our understanding of rebellion to teenage behavior and blatant acts of evil. It has been my experience that the most deceptive forms of rebellion are the nice or religious kind. I'll never forget how God taught me this when Princess Diana of England was killed in an auto accident. Many were in mourning over her death. I too was sad. She seemed kind and had done a great deal of charity in her public life. Yet in my grief, I sensed error.

I questioned the Lord why I felt this way. God showed me in the Book of Revelation how the inhabitants of the world and their leaders would mourn and weep over the death of the woman called Babylon (Rev. 17:2; 18:1–19). She had brought prosperity and success; therefore, they were saddened by her death. Yet in the same book two prophets of God who preached righteousness are put to death, and those who dwell on the earth will rejoice over them and make merry (Rev. 11:1–10).

The world sorrows over the death of Babylon, but rejoices over the death of the prophets. I witnessed a measure of this when

Diana died. Both small and great mourned. Then I thought about her private life. By her own admittance there had been several extramarital affairs as well as other ungodly ways of life.

I then thought, *But God, she did so much good.* I did not realize *good* can often have a self-serving agenda of its own.

God spoke something to my heart that changed my viewpoint drastically. "John, Eve was not drawn to the *evil* side of the tree of the knowledge of good and evil. She was drawn to the *good* side."

I rehearsed the verse in my mind: "So when the woman saw that the tree was good . . . that it was pleasant . . . " (Gen. 3:6).

God then spoke these words I will never forget: "John, there is a good that is very rebellious to My authority."

I then realized there is an "evil" rebellion, and there is a "good" rebellion. Both, however, are rebellion, and both are an affront to God's authority. Most in the church would never fall for the "evil" rebellion. Drug abuse, organized crime, wild drinking parties are too obvious. But today many in the church could be swayed with the "good" rebellion . . . Eve was. She was not tempted to be like Satan. She was tempted to be like God.

Hananiah's prophecy of restoration and peace seemed good, and his word could be confirmed through Scripture found in the Torah that was not applied correctly. Still, it was not what God was saying. Looking from our perspective it is easy to see why it did not please God. Hindsight, they say, is always 20/20, especially when you have the benefit of reading God's viewpoint through the Bible. We must remember, these people did not have hindsight. They really believed they were right with God. They were deceived and therefore easy targets for further deception and rebellion by counterfeit prophetic words. After their judgment, hindsight said:

> The visions of your prophets were false and worthless; they did not expose your sin to ward off your captivity. The oracles they gave you were false and misleading.
> —LAMENTATIONS 2:14, NIV

Not only were the blatantly rebellious affected, but also the numerous others who inhabited Jerusalem at that time. Some were young, some were wounded, others were not instructed in the statutes of the Lord. These were easy prey for deception. On these people the false prophets had the greatest impact. If these prophets had proclaimed repentance and righteousness they could have led many back to God. But their counterfeit oracles of peace, restoration, and prosperity had the opposite effect. It influenced some to rebel while strengthening the already present rebellion in others. That is why God said to Hananiah, "You have taught rebellion against the LORD."

This is exactly what the word given to the pastor's daughter did. She was young and easily influenced, especially by someone with a well-known and respected ministry. Even though the word sounded spiritual and made her feel special, it encouraged rebellion and led her astray and out from under her parents' authority.

AN INSUBORDINATE PROPHET?

We've examined a number of examples in which rebellion was sown through "prophetic words." The reason for its frequency and apparent success is this: Once a word is given that appeals to the desires of the discontented or covetous, it is very hard for them to reject it. It takes spiritual fortitude to reject what would bring happiness in order to embrace what is difficult. Often the ways of God will not initially or at all bring pleasure or comfort to our flesh! Jesus says, "Narrow is the gate and difficult is the way which leads to life, and there are few who find it" (Matt. 7:14).

When I served as an associate pastor in the 1980s, I came to know a man who was married and had two boys. He was at every service and was always anxious to talk about the things of God. He seemed very passionate for the Lord. He was placed in a position of serving that would help develop any calling on his life; however, he was unfaithful with almost every task assigned to him. He only did the things that brought him recognition or the platform to do what he liked. As time went on I noticed areas in his personal life that were alarming. He was extremely harsh and demanding on his wife and children.

I confronted him a few times about his personal life and his lack of commitment when asked to do things that were not glamorous, but he did not listen. His commitment greatly waned, and eventually he shared with me that he had gotten a prophetic word that he was a prophet. That explained his rebellion. Why would a mighty prophet be called on to submit to any local pastoral authority? He only submitted when he agreed with what he was called on to do, and that is not submission! He quit his job and left the church group to pursue his ministry. He refused to work and found no resting place, so he moved from group to group.

He became harsher and more headstrong, until a few months later the police were called to his home. No charges were pressed, but it gave me an opportunity to talk with him. I confronted him with the issues in his life I felt had to be dealt with. I warned him they would continue until he submitted himself to a pastor. I told him until this happened any call on his life would not come forth.

This greatly angered him. His rebellion became increasingly open. He told people that his ministry would be very well known no matter what I had said to him. He warned me that one day I'd stand on a platform with him and have to apologize. (This was from a word he was given). Ten years have passed. His wife and children have left him, and now they are divorced.

The "prophetic word" given to him was pleasant and promised recognition. I am sure he rejoiced when he was proclaimed a prophet of the Lord. Yet what was the fruit? It strengthened the rebellion in his life and planted a harvest of pride and insubordination. I could no longer help him. He no longer listened to counsel from the Scriptures. He had become a law unto himself. He was a prophet that would not submit to anyone! How sad.

THE ATTITUDE THAT KEEPS US FROM BEING MISLED

I want to repeat this point. Only a disciple of Jesus rejects what would bring happiness or recognition in order to embrace what is difficult. The life of a believer is never easy, and those who seek comfort and recognition are destined for error. They can easily be led away into rebellion, especially if it is tagged with "Thus saith the Lord."

Moses is an example of one who embraced truth over comfort

and recognition. His testimony stands as a witness to New Testament believers. We are told he forfeited the temporary pleasures and riches of Egypt and chose to suffer affliction alongside the people of God. He thought it better to suffer for the sake of the Messiah than to own the rewards of selfishness. (See Hebrews 11:25–26, NLT.)

Paul made a statement that should be taught to every new believer: "For to you it has been granted on behalf of Christ, not only to believe in Him, but also to suffer for His sake" (Phil. 1:29). On his first journey as an apostle sent to the Gentiles he ministered in four cities in Asia before returning to his home church. The four cities were Antioch, Iconium, Lystra, and the final city being Derbe. Once he and his team left Derbe:

> . . . they returned to Lystra, Iconium, and Antioch, strengthening the souls of the disciples, exhorting them to continue in the faith, and saying, "We must through many tribulations enter the kingdom of God."
>
> —ACTS 14:21–22

Notice he did not strengthen these young believers with a prosperity or success seminar. Nor did he tell them of the blessings available to them. Bear in mind these are his final words, and it is certain he chose them carefully. He did not know if he would be back and wanted to leave them with words that would guard and keep them from deception. He wanted their focus correct. "Don't watch for opportunities for ease and comfort," Paul was saying, "but rather expect hardship on your journey with God."

Paul's attitude is seen as he writes to the believers of Corinth: "For Christ's sake, I delight in weaknesses, in insults, in hardships, in persecutions, in difficulties" (2 Cor. 12:10, NIV). Is this the attitude we hear today? Do we delight in these things? Because of his pure devotion to Jesus he was able to resist any counsel or prophecy that might deter him from obedience.

When Agabus prophesied Paul would be chained and turned over to the Gentiles in Jerusalem, it created quite a stir among his companions and other believers present:

Now when we heard these things, both we and those from that place pleaded with him not to go up to Jerusalem. Then Paul answered, "What do you mean by weeping and breaking my heart? For I am ready not only to be bound, but also to die at Jerusalem for the name of the Lord Jesus." So when he would not be persuaded, we ceased, saying, "The will of the Lord be done."

—ACTS 21:12–14

Pure devotion to Jesus will keep us from receiving words that teach rebellion and lead us astray. Contrast Paul with our present time. Today many leave churches, ministry teams, or other realms in which God has placed them because they got a word from a fellow believer or prophet. These words usually start with how great the calling is on their life, confirming their importance in the kingdom. Often these words come when they are experiencing hardship, pressures, or dryness in their present place or position. This makes them receptive at the time. The prophet picks this up and addresses it, often first through sympathy followed by the exciting and stimulating words that are exactly what they want to hear. These words pull them out of discomfort and place them in success, recognition, or comfort. We mistake this as the promotion of the Lord when it is often the easy path of disobedience.

Most often rebellion is deceptively subtle. We only look for it in the blatant. But it is also found in the self-willed or willful. Out of ignorance many disciples are falling headlong into the pit of insubordination. The next few chapters will examine with great clarity how this operates unchecked.

We open ourselves up to trouble when the church tolerates what God has not ordained.

10

THE OPERATION
OF JEZEBEL

It was a Saturday evening during the summer of 1997. I was preparing to minister Sunday morning. In prayer the Lord spoke, "Go to the Book of Revelation, chapter 2." As I did I came to the church of Thyatira and read about a woman named Jezebel. I was strongly impressed that I was to minister along these lines.

I was not thrilled about this subject, though. I tried to avoid it by asking the Lord for another topic He might possibly want me to speak on. I didn't want to preach on this subject because often it is preached as a form of control or abuse. Many who teach on what has been termed a "Jezebel spirit" use it to beat up women in the church. I knew this was not what Jesus was communicating. Finally, after some struggle with my emotions, I submitted to this leading and received His message for the next morning. I admit what He revealed to me turned my thinking around.

THE MESSAGE APPLIED TODAY

First, let's discuss this letter to the church of Thyatira. This was an historic church in Asia during the time period when the Scriptures of the New Testament were written. The message was directed to their precise circumstances. However, God would have never allowed it in the Scriptures if it did not have some present or prophetic application. I believe it has something for us today.

Though it contains specifics, such as the name of a church and a specific woman, it is not confined to these details. The Lord's message and context could apply to a man or a group of people just as easily as to a woman. I don't believe gender is the issue here. The importance is found in what this woman was doing. The deception in which she operated disturbed and angered the Lord so deeply that He pointed it out to all. In this lies the prophetic message for us today. Let's read from the beginning:

> And to the angel of the church in Thyatira write . . .
>
> —REVELATION 2:18

If you study the way Jesus began each message to the seven churches, you'll find, "To the angel of the church of . . . " To understand who these angels are we need to examine the original text. The Greek word for *angel* is *aggelos*. This word means "a messenger." It is the same Greek word used to describe John the Baptist. "Behold, I send My messenger [*aggelos*] before Your face, who will prepare Your way before You" (Mark 1:2).

Jesus directs each of His messages to the seven churches through the *aggelos*. Just as God sent a message to His people through the prophet John prior to Jesus' first coming, I believe the heartbeat of His message to the church prior to His Second Coming is found in these seven letters.

NOT A MESSAGE FOR A DEAD CHURCH

Let's look specifically at this church of Thyatira:

> And to the angel of the church in Thyatira write, "These things says the Son of God, who has eyes like a flame of fire, and His feet like fine brass: I know your works, love, service, faith, and your patience; and as for your works, the last are more than the first."
>
> —REVELATION 2:18–19

110

I want to point out that this church was abundant with Christian works and love. They were active in service, and their faith and patience were real. In regard to works, they were more active than when they began. So we immediately see He was not speaking to a dead church. This church was an alive and active body of believers pressing into the things of God. Modern vernacular would describe this church as "on the cutting edge of what God is doing. It reaches out to the lost, has great teaching, and the gifts of the Spirit are in operation." This message is not for dead churches or believers. It is a specific warning to live ones.

Notice Jesus was described as one whose eyes are like a flame of fire. This denotes an intense ability to see through any darkness or outward veil to the very heart of the matter. If penned today, the verse might have compared His eyes to lasers. They pierce through the natural and obvious to expose the very root or motive. By all appearances, this church lacked nothing. Without discernment this body of believers would appear flawless, yet Jesus saw past the great works of this body and pointed out a very dangerous flaw. He warned:

> Nevertheless I have a few things against you, because you allow that woman Jezebel . . .
>
> —REVELATION 2:20

Immediately I recognized the name *Jezebel.* I did what I'd always done in the past and flipped over to 1 Kings to read the account of Queen Jezebel, wife of Ahab, king of Israel. In the past whenever I had studied or heard anyone teach on the "Jezebel spirit," the majority of content came from this queen in the Old Testament. This time as I turned my pages I heard the Spirit of God question me, "John, why are you going to that woman to learn what I'm saying to this church?"

I stopped and thought, *It is what I'm supposed to do. It is what everyone else does. That is how we learn the operation of this spirit.*

The Lord questioned me again, "John, if you want to learn about Joseph, the stepfather of Jesus, do you go to the Book of Genesis and study Joseph, the son of Jacob?"

Confused, I answered, "No."

The Lord then said, "The Joseph of Genesis and the Joseph of the New Testament have nothing in common except their name and their Jewish origin. Likewise the Jezebel of 1 and 2 Kings has nothing to do with the Jezebel in the Book of Revelation. John, everything you need to know about the operation of this woman in Thyatira is in Revelation. The other Jezebel of the Old Testament will only cloud and confuse the issue."

When I heard this, I was excited because I knew that now I'd be looking at it from the right perspective. I flipped back to Revelation and again read Jesus' words to this active church. As anticipated, the whole scenario took on a different light when the emphasis was off the Old Testament queen. Since then God has progressively revealed more about how this deceiving spirit works through both men and women, bringing deception to the church.

JEZEBEL IN THE CHURCH

Let's look at the message of Jesus to this dynamic church. Keep in mind that we are focusing on the *principles*, not the *specifics*. Let's look at what He is saying to us today:

> Nevertheless I have a few things against you, because you allow that woman Jezebel, who calls herself a prophetess, to teach and seduce My servants to commit sexual immorality and eat things sacrificed to idols. And I gave her time to repent of her sexual immorality, and she did not repent. Indeed I will cast her into a sickbed, and those who commit adultery with her into great tribulation, unless they repent of their deeds.
>
> —REVELATION 2:20–22

There are several key points we need to recognize. In this chapter I will list and briefly introduce each point. The next few chapters will cover these main points in depth. The first two points are not listed in order of their appearance in the verse for the sake of clarity and emphasis.

"... who calls herself a prophetess ... "

After being directed away from the Old Testament Jezebel, I returned to this scripture, and these words jumped off the page, impacting my spirit. I recognized them as a major piece in the puzzle of error wrought by this lady. She had assumed a position of ministry, that of a prophetess, without the Lord placing her in this office.

"I have a few things against you, because you allow that woman Jezebel ... "

This church permitted her to minister as a prophetess, even though Jesus did not recognize her as such. Another translation says the church "tolerated" her ministry (NIV). We open ourselves up to trouble when the church tolerates what God has not ordained.

"... to teach ... "

The Greek word for *teach* simply means "to impart instruction or to instill doctrine." This could be accomplished by example (through lifestyle) or by verbal or written communication.

"... and seduce ... "

The Greek word for *seduce* is *planao*. It is defined as "to cause to stray, to lead astray, to lead aside from the right way." It could be translated "deceive." This same Greek word was used by Jesus in Matthew 24:4, "Take heed that no one deceives you." In fact, this word appears forty-seven times in the New Testament and most often the word *deceived* is used. Let's see whom she deceives through her ministry.

"... My servants ... "

The Greek word for *servants* is the word *doulos*, the word Paul, Peter, James, and other of the Lord's disciples used for themselves. In the context of Scripture, it means "one who has willingly made himself a slave out of devotion to the Lord Jesus." This woman's counterfeit prophetic ministry deceived those who aggressively followed and served the Lord Jesus. Remember, Jesus warned that the latter-days false prophets would arise and deceive, if possible, His chosen ones.

This point cannot be overemphasized. The counterfeit prophetic is so deceptively close to the real that it targets those with strong commitments to the Lord.

". . . to commit fornication, and to eat things sacrificed unto idols"
(KJV)

The Greek word for *fornication* is *porneuo*, defined by Thayer's dictionary of Greek words as "to give oneself to unlawful sexual intercourse." It is further defined as "to be given to idolatry; the worship of idols; or to permit oneself to be drawn away by another into idolatry."[1] Jezebel was leading true servants of the Lord into fornication or idolatry by way of seduction or deception.

Whether this was physical or spiritual fornication is not the main issue. Throughout the Bible, God used terms of sexual immorality to describe Israel's unfaithful idolatry. He said Judah "defiled the land and committed adultery with stones and trees" (Jer. 3:9). In Ezekiel 6:9, God described His grief with His people: "I was crushed by their adulterous heart which has departed from Me, and by their eyes which play the harlot after their idols." Then again in Ezekiel 23:37 He said, "They have committed adultery with their idols." In the New Testament believers who seek a relationship with the world are compared to "adulterers and adulteresses" (James 4:4). These are but a few references. From them it is obvious Jezebel's adultery is not limited to physical sex.

The broader definition of adultery is also suggested by the terminology Jesus used to describe the consequences of Jezebel's ministry. "Indeed I will cast her into a sickbed, and those who commit adultery with her into great tribulation, unless they repent of their deeds" (Rev. 2:22). This woman had influence on a scale large enough for Jesus to call attention to its deceptive influence. I don't believe everyone she seduced actually shared a physical bed with her. Notice He said those who commit adultery with her were to repent of their "deeds" rather than of sexual immorality.

Still, let's not focus on the physical, but go to the root. A believer who commits sexual fornication has already committed spiritual fornication. The spiritual precedes and leads into the physical fornication. Conversely, the one who commits spiritual fornication has not necessarily committed physical. There are believers who wouldn't dream of committing physical adultery or fornication. They have set their wills never to do so. They would feel exempt from these words of Jesus due to the absence of physical sexual immorality. Yet a number of these Christians might easily have been drawn away into spiritual adultery or idolatry because they lacked or rejected knowledge. This is the root Jesus addresses.

THE DEPTHS OF SATAN'S DECEPTION

Though our society and churches differ from those in Jezebel's day, the motive behind what Jezebel was doing has remained intact. Idolatry today takes on different shapes and forms; nevertheless, the same forces still lurk behind it. I believe this is the reason we find this specific account in the Scriptures. It is a prophetic warning that certainly applies to us today!

In the early stages of this book I heard the Lord say, "You will face resistance in writing this book for it exposes a major inroad of the enemy into My church."

I questioned this, thinking, *Surely this can't be true. There are other ways and means the enemy has developed that are more effective.* Then I read what Jesus said about the counterfeit prophetic ministry:

> But I also have a message for the rest of you in Thyatira who have not followed this false teaching ("deeper truths," as they call them—depths of Satan, really.) I will ask nothing more of you except that you hold tightly to what you have until I come.
>
> REVELATION 2:24–25, NLT

I realized the severity of this false ministry. Jesus called this teaching the "depths of Satan." The next few chapters examine more closely just how detrimental it can be to assume the position of a prophet without God's appointment.

Appointment by God is so
necessary that even Jesus did
not assume His position of
leadership but was appointed
by the Father.

11

SELF OR GOD APPOINTED

In the eighties I was one of eleven assistant pastors on staff at a church of approximately seven thousand members. During a staff meeting a situation was brought up about a man in the church. Though he hadn't been a member very long, each of us knew who he was because he was very active. He sat in the front section each service, faithfully attended prayer meetings, and was active in the young adults ministry. It seemed his time was given to much prayer, study of the Word, and church attendance. But something wasn't right.

As we met together a number of incidents surfaced. After some investigation we realized that in a short period of time many had left the church due to this man's involvement in their lives. The senior pastor told another pastor and myself to deal with the situation immediately.

But it didn't make sense, because during worship I saw him weep, during the preaching of the Word he was receptive and eager, and in other areas he was active. I was young in the ministry and confused about why this was happening. So I prayed, "Lord, please show me what we're dealing with. This man really seems to love You, yet the fruit of his life is not good."

I heard the Holy Spirit immediately answer, "He's a self-appointed prophet."

117

A few days later I met with the other pastor and this man after a service. We discussed with him the situations in question. He shared how God had given him prophetic messages for the people whom we brought to his attention. He was adamant that his words and visions were from the Lord, insisting he had to speak what God had given him to speak.

After some time it was apparent our conversation was going nowhere, so I confronted him. "In prayer God spoke to me and said you are a self-appointed prophet." I explained that this opened him and those under his influence to deception. Though he didn't like what I said, we could see the words had impacted him. We gave him some guidelines to which he reluctantly agreed.

But the truth is he was offended by the conversation and found a way to continue his "prophetic ministry" outside our guidelines. Within weeks he was arrested for breaking the law. When he was released from jail he continued his "prophetic ministry" to small groups he had drawn to himself in homes. Later he and his wife divorced due to intense marital conflict.

Years later when the Holy Spirit opened my eyes to Jezebel in the Book of Revelation, this situation and many others came into focus. Let's reexamine Jesus' words:

> Nevertheless I have a few things against you, because you allow that woman Jezebel, who calls herself a prophetess . . .
> —REVELATION 2:20

Notice the phrase, "who calls herself a prophetess." The night God opened my eyes to this portion of Scripture these words went off inside of me like a bomb. I saw this woman assuming a position of spiritual authority that God hadn't given her. In the process, she deceived those under her influence. To understand, let's discuss spiritual offices of ministry.

THE DIFFERENCE BETWEEN CALLED AND APPOINTED

Many Americans have difficulties with kingdom principles. We live in a democratic society of free enterprise, which varies vastly from a kingdom. A kingdom has a reigning king by virtue of birthright. A democracy elects its rulers. In the free enterprise system, leadership is available to all with abilities and talents who put their minds to it. But this is not the way of God's kingdom.

When Jesus was raised from the dead He was placed in authority over the church, and "He Himself gave some to be apostles, some prophets, some evangelists, and some pastors and teachers" (Eph. 4:11). Jesus appointed these offices of service. No one else can place a human being in these positions of authority except the Lord, and He does it through the Spirit of God.

Whenever we assume a position of authority without God's appointment we are exalting ourselves. This includes those who are called but have yet to be appointed. Persons who commission themselves will ultimately serve themselves since the grace of God is not on them for that position. They will develop self-serving methods and agendas. Paul warns, "For I say, through the grace given to me, to everyone who is among you, not to think of himself more highly than he ought to think" (Rom. 12:3).

The Book of Hebrews affirms the importance of not assuming a position of spiritual leadership. First the writer describes how a spiritual leader is "selected from among men and is appointed to represent them" (Heb. 5:1, NIV). Then he points out, "No one takes this honor upon himself, he must be called by God" (v. 4, NIV). Appointment by God is so necessary that even Jesus did not assume His position of leadership but was appointed by the Father. "So also Christ did not glorify Himself to become High Priest" (v. 5).

Listen to Paul's description of himself: "Paul, a bondservant of Jesus Christ, called to be an apostle, separated to the gospel of God" (Rom. 1:1). Notice he first mentions "called" and then mentions "separated." Paul was called as an apostle from the foundation of the world though he was not placed in this office the moment He was saved. There was a period of testing when he submitted to the church leadership at Antioch. This test lasted years. From his own experience he wrote these instructions for leaders: "But let these also first be tested; then let them serve" (1 Tim. 3:10).

Another word for *separated* is *chosen*. Jesus said, "For many are called, but few are chosen" (Matt. 22:14). In other words, many are called to positions of ministry, but only a small percentage pass the test and fulfill the requirements to be chosen or separated.

Paul's life established a scriptural pattern for today. During his first years in Antioch Paul did not occupy a fivefold office (Eph. 4:11). Instead, he served in the ministry of helps, supporting leadership already in place. Once Paul passed the test of faithfulness in the ministry of helps, he was promoted to the office of teacher (2 Tim. 1:11; Acts 13:1). We can see how Paul's ministry followed the Lord's divine order of offices and positions of service. The Bible says, "And God has appointed these in the church: first apostles, second prophets, third teachers, after that . . . helps . . ." (1 Cor. 12:28).

Not only would Paul be tested in the realm of helps but in the office of teacher as well. When Paul was promoted from teacher to apostle we again see how God chooses and separates those that He wants to fill certain offices or positions.

> Now in the church that was at Antioch there were certain prophets and teachers: Barnabas, Simeon who was called Niger, Lucius of Cyrene, Manaen who had been brought up with Herod the tetrarch, and Saul.
>
> —ACTS 13:1

Notice Saul, later named Paul, is listed among the teachers and prophets in the church of Antioch.

Continuing to read we find:

> As they ministered to the Lord and fasted, the Holy Spirit said, "Now separate to Me Barnabas and Saul for the work to which I have called them."
>
> —ACTS 13:2

Notice the Holy Spirit spoke, "Now separate to Me . . . " The time had come. It was not a week early or a week late. The time was now! And it was the Lord who determined both the timing and who was to be separated. For years Paul was aware there was an apostolic call on his life. It was revealed three days after his encounter with Jesus on the road to Damacus (Acts 9:15). Now Jesus had separated the one He had called so many years earlier. Paul had faithfully served without promoting himself. Later Paul admonished, "Moreover it is required in stewards that one be found faithful" (1 Cor. 4:2).

Notice the Lord used the established leadership of the church in which Paul had faithfully labored. Likewise these elders had been appointed in the same manner. Continuing we find:

> Then, having fasted and prayed, and laid hands on them, they sent them away. So, being sent out by the Holy Spirit, they went . . .
>
> —ACTS 13:3–4

Notice the third verse, "they sent them. . . . " The established leadership sent Paul and Barnabas. Then look at the next verse: "So, being sent out by the Holy Spirit . . . " Jesus appointed and separated Paul and Barnabas by the Holy Spirit through the established leadership. Bottom line, Jesus did it.

Notice Jesus did not use the prophetic intercessory prayer group of Antioch nor did He send Paul and Barnabas to a prophetic conference in another city or across town to another church where Paul was not submitted. God did not use an individual in the congregation with spiritual gifts to set these men in leadership.

The Lord used the authority He'd established through the church in Antioch. This is why God warns, "Do not lay hands on anyone hastily" (1 Tim. 5:22). The Contemporary English Version clarifies what it meant to lay hands on someone: "Don't be too quick to accept people into the service of the Lord by placing your hands on them." Leadership monitors the faithfulness of those who serve in the church. When God speaks to their hearts to appoint, they have confidence that it is the Lord's appointment. This is the Lord's method of appointing individuals to positions of leadership.

SENT BY GOD, MAN, OR SELF?

Today we have men and women in pulpits and congregations who consider themselves prophets or prophetess, yet are not. Often they have appointed themselves or been appointed by someone outside the leadership of the church they attend. They may have prophetic gifts operating in their lives, or they may have a genuine call to that office, but are not yet appointed. God declared:

> I have not sent these prophets, yet they ran. I have not spoken to them, yet they prophesied.
>
> —JEREMIAH 23:21

I remember my time period of testing. I served on the staff of a church for over four years. My responsibilities included taking care of my pastor, his family, and the guests. It was my place in the ministry of helps. As time passed I became anxious. I wanted to be in the fivefold ministry. I knew I was called, so I used my vacations to travel and develop my ministry. Some friends encouraged me to move into traveling ministry full time. This and other influences caused me to contemplate resigning my position of serving. Returning on a plane from a ministry outing to the Philippines I read, "There was a man sent from God, whose name was John" (John 1:6).

The words "sent from God" jumped off the page. Suddenly I heard the Lord question, "Do you want to be sent by John Bevere, or sent from God?"

I said, "Sent from God!"

He said, "Good. If you send yourself you'll go in your authority. If I send you, you'll go in My authority!"

He showed me that if I sent myself I'd still see results because of the gifts He'd placed on my life. But the results would not carry the same eternal benefit for those I touched—or for myself.

The Lord showed me how Moses headed toward this same error. The Book of Acts records that "Moses was learned in all the wisdom of the Egyptians, and was mighty in words and deeds" (Acts 7:22). From infancy he was raised in the king of Egypt's home. He was trained as a prince. His leadership skills were learned at the finest schools in the world. Not only was the hand of God on him for leadership, but the gifts in his life were honed in these schools.

We learn, "Now when he was forty years old, it came into his heart to visit his brethren, the children of Israel . . . For he supposed that his brethren would have understood that God would deliver them by his hand" (Acts 7:23–25). The Scriptures make it clear that Moses knew in his heart he was the deliverer God would use to break the bondage of Egypt from his brethren. But it is one thing to be called and another thing to be appointed.

Moses confused the developed gifts in his life coupled with the calling in his heart as God's appointment. He went out to free Israel and failed. In his own authority he was only able to help one fellow Hebrew by killing a single Egyptian, a far cry from delivering a nation. This caused him to flee for his life. After forty years God appointed and sent him in divine authority. Then Moses delivered Israel and saw the entire Egyptian calvary buried under the Red Sea!

BROKENNESS: A REQUIREMENT FOR SERVICE

Moses had enough wisdom not to force the call of God after he had seen the futility of his own efforts. Getting ahead of God's timing seems to be a struggle common to those called to ministry. The wise will draw back, allowing the breaking and training process of the Lord to run its course. Those unwise strive against His process and press into their ministries. But Jesus warns:

> Whoever falls on this stone will be broken; but on whomever it falls, it will grind him to powder.
> —MATTHEW 21:44

Jesus is the Stumbling Stone, and His breaking process could be compared to a trainer breaking a war-horse. A horse is not fit for battle until his will is broken. Though he may be stronger, swifter and more gifted than all those around him, he cannot serve until his will is broken. To be broken does not mean to be weakened. It means your will is completely submitted to the will of your master. In the horse's case, its master is the rider. If the horse is successfully broken and trained he can be trusted in war. In the heat of battle as arrows or bullets fly he will not flinch. While axes, swords, and guns are raised in battle he will not deviate from his master's desires. He will stay in firm submission to his master, void of any attempt to protect or benefit himself.

This breaking process is unique to each individual and determined by the Lord Himself. He is the only one who knows when this process is complete! I remember His breaking process in my life. All too often I fully believed I was ready and fit for service. I would declare with confidence, "I am fully submitted to Your authority. I know I am ready for the ministry You have called me to." Yet the wise in heart knew I wasn't broken yet. Sure enough, I'd go through another bout, all the while struggling for my rights.

Just as with horses, our breaking process deals with submission to authority. This can be God's direct or delegated authority. It does not matter, for all authority is from Him (Rom. 13:1–2). God knows the perfect process for each of us.

God set up two kings who illustrate the breaking process—Saul and David. Saul represented the people's desire in a king, accurately reflecting what their rebellious hearts cried out for. Saul never went through a breaking process. His life is a tragic example of an unbroken man who was given authority and power. Saul used his authority and God-given gifts to further his own purposes.

On the other hand, David was God's choice. He went through several years of breaking and training. The majority of it revolved around King Saul, the authority under which God had placed David. He was severely tested, but when God saw that His vessel was broken and submitted, He placed him in authority. Even though he made mistakes, David always remained tender and faithful to the authority of God.

In contrast, Saul obeyed God when it fit in with his plans or agenda but would sway when it didn't. He would carry the word of the Lord with his own motives attached. Saul was confronted by the prophet Samuel for disobedience and rebuked with these words: "Stubbornness *is as* iniquity and idolatry" (1 Sam. 15:23).

Samuel linked stubbornness directly to idolatry. Notice that the words "is as" are in italics. This presentation is common in the King James version when the words did not appear in the original text but were added by the translators to lend clarity. A more accurate translation would have used only the word "is."[1]

The text then would read, "Stubbornness is iniquity and idolatry." This translation is in harmony with the context. It is one thing to be *like* idolatry but quite another to *be* idolatry. Why is stubbornness idolatry? Because it is direct insubordination to God's authority. It is when one makes himself master. He serves the idol of self-will.

Our democratic society is a breeding ground for insubordination. Because of this we have lost sight of what it means to submit to authority. True submission never wavers. Yet today we only submit when we agree. If authority goes against our will or direction, we disobey or grudgingly go along with it until a better option presents itself. This makes us especially vulnerable to deception and the counterfeit prophetic ministry.

In the Book of Revelation the woman Jezebel assumed a position of authority—prophetess—and then taught and seduced God's servants into idolatry. This bred stubbornness and insubordination toward God's kingdom authority.

Let me make one more comment about the man mentioned at the beginning of this chapter. Though he cried in services it became obvious he was not broken and contrite. He was insubordinate to those in authority at the church. This stubbornness also seduced others into idolatry—insubordination. Though his fruit was evident to the mature, the young, weak, and wounded sheep were drawn to him. Remember, Paul said to believers, "Also from among yourselves men will rise up, speaking perverse things, to draw away the disciples after themselves" (Acts 20:30).

In the next chapter we will see the ease with which self-appointed prophets draw others out from under true spiritual authority. It is so subtle that without the proper foundation of the Word of God anyone can easily fall prey.

Without God-given authority
you must usurp authority
through deception.

12

THE STING OF JEZEBEL

Not too long ago I ministered in the Northern part of the United States. It was my second series of meetings with this congregation, which had grown to approximately one thousand members in a town of less than one hundred thousand people. No other independent church in this area had grown to this size. The pastor is a passionate man whom I remembered as an effective leader.

The meetings held the previous year had been wonderful. The people were eager to receive the Word of God. The atmosphere was easy to preach in, and the services bore much fruit. I was excited to see what God would do at my second set of meetings.

The first service was Sunday morning. I was caught off guard by the difference I sensed in the atmosphere from the year before. Instead of liberty while I preached, I felt as though I were plowing through a thick wall of rebellion. I was baffled and questioned, "Is this the same congregation I stood before a year ago?" The change was so pronounced, I was almost certain this church had been affected by some type of divination.

I didn't address it in the morning service, but I sought the Lord's counsel that afternoon in my hotel room. I sensed a confirmation of what I'd sensed that morning. This church had been stung by a Jezebel spirit. I didn't know whether it had been released when

127

someone visited the church or if it had arisen from among the members. I only knew it was there. The previous structure of order and authority in this church had suffered a devastating blow from some type of counterfeit prophetic. I was keenly aware that I was to address it head on that night in the service.

I preached from Jesus' message to the church of Thyatira in Revelation. It was easy to sense the rebellion and resistance in the atmosphere. It had only increased since that morning. Yet I felt a divine authority on the Word and was aware the message was literally cutting through the resistant atmosphere. I sensed a weakening of the rebellion as the divination was exposed by the light of God's Word.

After over an hour of preaching I asked those who knew they were under the influence or attack of a Jezebel spirit to stand to their feet. I clearly outlined their first step to freedom as repentance from the rebellion into which they'd been seduced. I was amazed when over 70 percent of the church responded. After leading the people in prayer, there was a clearing in the atmosphere that was both liberating and thrilling.

After service the pastor hurried me back to his office. I knew we were going to have a serious talk, but I had no idea what he was going to say. He closed the office door, sat down, and breathed a heavy sigh of relief.

"John," he said. "Now I want to tell you what I've been going through." He had said nothing to me up to this point. His face was solemn as he shared, "I have had about twenty hours of sleep in the last thirty days."

I looked at him and could tell he was exhausted. "Why?" I asked. "What has been going on?"

He said, "It all began five months ago when I had a well-known prophetic minister in our church. As you know, we've been in a building program. Well, this person stood before my congregation and gave some personal words, then said, 'Thus saith the Lord, "You are building too small."' The minister said the Lord was saying we needed to double the size of the building because of the great things He was going to do.

"John, I scrapped eighty-five thousand dollars worth of architectural drawings, plans, and other fees to start over. I wanted to build the sanctuary God said we were to build."

He continued, "That's not all. This person knew that my worship team and I planned to produce a CD eventually and said that God wanted it out in the next six months. My worship team was very excited. In order to accomplish this, it meant the purchase of twenty-five thousand dollars' worth of recording equipment. It was really not a wise move for us at the time, but how could I go against God's desire? So we spent the money and now have a CD that hasn't done much."

He shared how a few months later his overseer, who pastors a large church in the South, flew up and sat him down and told him what he was doing was way out of their range. He counseled against taking on a building of that size because he believed it was asking for trouble.

He continued, "John, I knew my pastor was right when he told me I was building too big. I felt the weight of it lift from me, but that is when the big problems began. Because these words were given in front of both my members and leadership, they now thought I was in unbelief and disobedience to the word of the Lord. I tried to explain my position to the congregation, but this didn't help. It was as though all godly wisdom had been thrown to the wind in the wake of the excitement of the prophecy."

He paused then said, "It's as though that one night of ministry stripped me of almost every bit of authority I held as a pastor, a leader, and as a man of God. Tonight God restored it."

The next day the pastor and I talked at length and in greater detail about what had transpired in the meeting five months earlier. Another point of interest was raised. He shared that they had welcomed this minister as a friend, but this minister was upset at not being acknowledged in the bulletin as one standing in prophetic office. The guest minister even brought up the omission when introduced before the congregation. Scriptural pattern is that God—not man—validates His prophets and servants. One who is great among men often is not in the kingdom of God. Recall Jesus said, "Woe to you when all men speak well of you, for so did their fathers to the false prophets" (Luke 6:26).

Jesus said the Jezebel of Thyatira called herself a prophetess. She took the position upon herself and then demanded the recognition of man. Jezebel was obviously a good communicator or she would not have been able to draw so many into rebellion through her teaching. No matter how well we communicate, if our motive is to draw others to ourselves we will inevitably produce the wrong fruit.

Bigger churches and popular CDs at first sound like a God idea. These types of words produce excitement and provide an appealing vision to rally around. The only problem is the people rallied around the counterfeit, while God's divine authority and will were perverted. Their eyes were diverted and distracted from what was before them and from the leader who faithfully labored among them to embrace the words of one who did not. Unknowingly they were led away from God's authority. I wish I could say this is an isolated incident, but I've seen it happen with other churches as well.

THE JEZEBEL MINISTRY OUTSIDE THE PULPITS

The Jezebel of Thyatira influenced others by way of a deceiving spirit. It was subtle and seductive in nature. These images describe the methods of present-day self-appointed prophets regardless of whether they are male or female. Often servants of the Lord are led into insubordination or other forms of modern idolatry by the Jezebel form of the prophetic. What is most alarming is the fact most do not realize they've been drawn into error until much later.

Jezebel's influence is not confined to the pulpit. Most often it sits in the congregation. Frequently you will find it in settings where hungry believers are outside corporate services, such as special meetings, Bible studies, prayer groups, and so on. Individuals under its influence often appear highly spiritual. They give the impression of hours in prayer and constant progressive revelation. You might be tempted to think of them as more spiritually discerning than the pastor. They assure you their "maturity" is the very reason they are there to intercede for the pastor. (This is not to imply that all those who pray diligently are Jezebels.)

While in their presence you may feel like your spiritual life pales in comparison as they relay the many things God has told or shown them through prayer, visions, or dreams. You find yourself feeling almost unspiritual or backslidden in comparison. If there is any insecurity in your relationship with God you will find yourself cowering spiritually before them. This is exactly what the Jezebel ministry wants. It is very strong and longs to intimidate you into submission to its way of thinking.

If you are already strong it will try another tactic. It will flatter you and raise you up to its level of pride. "The Lord has shown me you're very spiritual . . . even more so than your husband." This may or may not be the case, but it doesn't change the authority structure in the house. The goal is to pull you out from under the protective authority in which God puts you. It will isolate you and cause you to be dependent on them for revelations from God.

GIFTS VS. AUTHORITY

Again it is important to emphasize that you can have spiritual gifting and insight, but that does not mean God has set you in a position of governing authority. God gives gifts to men by His Spirit, but the governing offices are established by the Lord Jesus. We get into trouble when we mistake gifts for offices. Often those who have established themselves as prophets or prophetesses have a genuine gifting in that area. They have developed these gifts and can perceive or see into people's lives. But when a gift is not submitted to the lordship of Jesus and therefore His governing authority, the gift is submitted to the will of self. In this setting it is easy for the gift to be misused or perverted in the person's development because the motives become self-serving. Self-exaltation perverts the gift. They mistake the gift for authority. Just because we are gifted does not mean we are ready for or have authority.

In the Book of Numbers we find an excellent example of this in the actions of Moses' big sister and brother.

> Miriam and Aaron began to talk against Moses because of his Cushite wife, for he had married a Cushite. "Has the LORD spoken only through Moses?" they asked. "Hasn't he also spoken through us?" And the LORD heard this.
>
> —NUMBERS 12:1–2, NIV

They believed he'd made a mistake and felt free to speak against him as if in authority over him. It is uncertain if they spoke these words in the privacy of their tents or shared them openly with others. Regardless of the extent, it is certain the Lord heard them.

Their words and intentions were very offensive to God. In anger God summoned all three before His presence and then questioned Miriam and Aaron, "Why then were you not afraid to speak against my servant Moses?" (Num. 12:1–8, NIV). Then His presence lifted, leaving Miriam leprous.

How did these siblings of Moses make such a grave error in judgment? The answer is revealed through their proud words: "Has the LORD indeed spoken only through Moses? Has He not spoken through us also?" (Num. 12:2). God did speak through Miriam and Aaron. Both were supernaturally gifted, and Aaron was a priest. Yet they used the gifting in their lives as justification to elevate themselves above the authority God placed over them. If God had not swiftly exposed this folly, they would have misled numerous others with the same reasoning. They were judged before the entire congregation that all might fear. When they repented of this error, both were forgiven and restored.

Miriam and Aaron were not false prophets, but their error illustrates the difference between authority and gifts. If they would have persisted in their crusade they could have ended up as false prophets. We must realize that what is false does not necessarily begin that way.

Inspirational gifts are not grounds for self-promotion. Gifts do not necessarily mean you have God's empowering grace of authority. Without God-given authority you must usurp authority through deception. This means intentionally or unintentionally drawing others away from their God-given authority structure to empower the counterfeit.

SPREAD YOUR WINGS

The following example is one a pastor and his wife told me when I preached in their church. When they heard I was writing on this topic they were eager to share their pain in the hope of protecting others. In his own words, "This is one of those sad tales we wish we had not experienced."

This man of God has pastored a large church in a major city in the United States for more than thirty years. His head associate has been with him twenty-five, and most of his staff has been with him more than ten years. The church is very active in missions and helping the poor. To say the least, it is a stable and healthy church. He writes:

> Yes, we are a congregation that has been impacted by a woman who calls herself "a prophetess." Sadly, our former youth pastor whom I'd mentored for over fifteen years came under her control.
>
> Out of her own bitterness she began to chant words "from the Lord," like, "church without walls," "spread your wings," and "release." As a member of the congregation, she went among the people prophesying that the Lord wanted to release His people—inferring that somehow we, the leadership, had kept people from their ministry.
>
> The lie took hold of our youth pastor, creating discontent that sent him searching for other prophets to give him confirmation.
>
> Suddenly he began to talk of being called to the nations. Then he made contact with another so-called prophet [I know who this prophet is and he has a very well-known ministry] who gave him the generic "this is a new season in your life; it's time for change; God is broadening your vision, enlarging your ministry" word.
>
> These so-called confirming words from prophets closed his heart to our appeals. When confronted by leadership he became offended and defensive. He was certain that we were trying to keep him from following his "God-given dream."
>
> Finally, he listed his grandiose plans and went out from his homeland to follow his dream. He was Abraham, and his wife was Sarah. They were to go to a land where the promise would be fulfilled, establish a school of the arts and a retreat center for discouraged pastors, and follow his special calling to minorities, homosexuals, and others.

Three years later not one of these visions had come to pass. In the wake is a broken wife, four children at risk, another young man from our home church estranged from his family, and a group of young people confused and angry. This is the harvest of a "Jezebel, who calls herself a prophetess."

When the youth pastor left the church, he went to labor alongside the well-known prophet who'd given him the word. The senior pastor shared with me how the prophetic word seemed to be the starting point of dialogue between the prophet and the youth pastor. Though this youth pastor left to minister with the prophet, shortly after his arrival this prophet left him behind to start a church in another state.

I had done four services at the senior pastor's church before I had any of this knowledge. I ministered on submission, forgiveness, and the fear of the Lord. On the last night I noticed the music pastor, who had been with this church for seven years, weeping on the senior pastor's shoulders. He and his wife embraced the senior pastor and his wife for quite some time.

The next day this music pastor brought me to the airport. He shared that he'd been given a similar word, "to spread his wings and go forth," by the same woman who has since left the church. He confessed that though he didn't leave (because his wife disagreed with it), this word had caused him to question his pastor continually. The relationship had been strained for years because his heart had withdrawn from the place he had been planted. These few words had lured him into insubordination and stubbornness. Though he hadn't physically left, a breach was created by this word! Hear God's warning to us:

> Now I urge you, brethren, note those who cause divisions and offenses, contrary to the doctrine which you learned, and avoid them. For those who are such do not serve our Lord Jesus Christ, but their own belly, and by smooth words and flattering speech deceive the hearts of the simple.
>
> —ROMANS 16:17–18

The words of this woman and the well-known prophet were flattering and smooth. The words sounded Holy Spirit inspired since they were laced with biblical terminology. However, they also planted seeds of pride in these men's hearts, proposing higher callings on their lives as though serving in their present capacity was something to be despised. The flattery revealed the discontentment already resident in their hearts. The words were not according to sound doctrine, but instead were patterned to be self-serving for these two associates.

The Scriptures dictate that only established elders, who know the lives of those they serve, should give release words. The senior pastor was in position to give these, not a disgruntled church member or a prophet from another state at an outside meeting. The flattery of the counterfeit confused their scriptural discernment and pulled them away from God's divine authority.

When I questioned the pastor about the woman who had given these words, I learned she was well known in the church with a reputation for accuracy. We've already learned that accuracy does not validate a "word"; fruit does. Hear what the Scriptures warn:

> Suppose there are prophets among you, or those who have dreams about the future, and they promise you signs or miracles, and the predicted signs or miracles take place. If the prophets then say, "Come, let us worship the gods of foreign nations," do not listen to them. The LORD your God is testing you to see if you love him with all your heart and soul. Serve only the LORD your God and fear him alone. Obey his commands, listen to his voice, and cling to him.
> —DEUTERONOMY 13:1–4, NLT

These prophets among the Israelites served the gods of foreign nations. They were their idols. An idol is nothing in itself. It is empowered by the covetousness in men's hearts. We've learned that stubbornness, which is rebellion, is a form of idolatry. How does this scripture apply to us today? If a word pulls you away from God's direct or delegated authority, do not heed it. Even if these words are accurate or come to pass, we are instructed not to listen to these prophets "for they encourage rebellion against the LORD your God" (Deut. 13:5, NLT).

I spoke with the above pastor at a later date. I was happy to learn the relationship between him and the music minister had been restored. "His loyalty is greater where he is serving than it ever has been before," he happily told me. The senior pastor also shared how this music minister had a heightened awareness of the counterfeit prophetic.

It is my prayer you see my purpose in these examples that you might learn and be warned by them. Paul wrote:

> All these events happened to them as examples for us. They were written down to warn us, who live at the time when this age is drawing to a close.
> —1 CORINTHIANS 10:11, NLT

I hope you will never experience the sting of the counterfeit prophetic. Paul warns us, "For there are many insubordinate, both idle talkers and deceivers . . . " (Titus 1:10). Oh, how that applies to us today! A single book could never contain all the accounts of deception from false prophets throughout church history who seduce with smooth and flattering words. Numerous people with genuine callings have been pulled away from the prescribed place of training God had placed them in.

These men and women are usually going through rough or dry times when Jezebel lures them out. Though America has enjoyed years free from physical persecution, God still has a prescribed way to train and strengthen us. You don't send soldiers to a comfortable spa-getaway to train them for war. You send them to boot camp where the training is tough and uncomfortable. This properly prepares them for future warfare. Many times the exciting and comfortable promises are not from God.

A false prophet uses his God-entrusted gifts to draw others to himself. A true prophet draws them to the heart of God.

13

KNOWING PROPHETS BY THEIR FRUIT

G od is preparing His latter-day prophetic ministers. It is a very necessary and important ministry with a crucial and timely task. It must turn the heart of God's people back to Him to prevent God from striking the earth with a curse (Mal. 4:5–6). Perhaps this is why the enemy has worked so hard to pervert and prevent this restoration. If our hearts are not turned back to God and His true holiness, then the church will not walk in God's glory as He promised:

> "I will dwell in them and walk among them. I will be their God, and they shall be My people." . . . Therefore, having these promises, beloved, let us cleanse ourselves from all filthiness of the flesh and spirit, perfecting holiness in the fear of God.
>
> —2 CORINTHIANS 6:16; 7:1

This promise of His glory was foreshadowed in the Old Testament by Israel's deliverance out of Egypt and to Mount Sinai. Egypt represents this world's system. Israel's exodus is an example of our deliverance from this temporal world through salvation. God told Israel, "I bore you on eagles' wings and *brought you to Myself*" (Exod. 19:4, emphasis added). Just as with them, He saved

us to bring us to Himself. What a wonderful revelation!
God then told Moses:

> Go to the people and consecrate them today and tomorrow,
> and let them wash their clothes. And let them be ready for the
> third day. For on the third day the LORD will come down
> upon Mount Sinai in the sight of all the people.
>
> —EXODUS 19:10–11

To consecrate simply means "to set apart." God was saying, "I brought you out of Egypt; now you must get Egypt out of you!" A part of the preparation process was accomplished by the washing of their clothes, thus removing the traces of Egypt in preparation for His glory. Likewise, we are told to cleanse ourselves of all filthiness of the flesh and spirit. This is the cleansing of our garments of flesh and spirit to remove the stench of worldly desires. This purifies our desires that we might behold Him, for without holiness no one will see the Lord (Heb. 12:14).

On the third day God promised to reveal His glory to the children of Israel. This promise was not isolated to them but also applies to us, for in 2 Peter 3:8 we learn that one of God's days is a thousand of our years. For two days, or two thousand years, the church's responsibility has been to consecrate itself for the coming of His glory. On the beginning of the third day (the third thousand-year period), He will come in His glory [this is when Christ will come and reign a thousand years in His glorified body (Rev. 20:4)].

Just as Moses was the prophet who called God's people to consecration before His visitation, so again the latter-day Elijah prophets will proclaim this message prior to His Second Coming. We are near the end of the second day! Yet the church is still soiled by the spirit of the world. It is filled with so many who long for the comforts, pleasures, and benefits of this world's system—the very Egypt that once enslaved us. With divided hearts many have desired salvation and the blessings of Jesus, all the while longing for the world. They are physically in the desert, but their hearts remain in Egypt.

This condition was prophesied by the apostle Paul. He described terrible times in the latter days (2 Tim. 3:1, NIV). Men would profess Christianity and yet still love themselves and their money. They would be proud, disobedient, ungrateful, unloving, unforgiving, slanderers, lacking in the fear of God and self-control, and loving pleasure more than God. "They will act as if they are religious, but they will reject the power that could make them godly" (2 Tim. 3:1–5, NLT).

To remedy this condition, God is sending the prophetic to reveal our true condition that we as a church might turn back to God. In order to accomplish this it is imperative that the prophetic comes forth pure and undefiled. We are poised on the threshold of destruction, for if the prophetic is polluted, we will not be prepared. Satan knows judgment begins in the house of God, and he wants us to be judged. He does this by fueling the fire of iniquity and covetousness. Jesus foresaw this and warned that in our day "many false prophets will rise up and deceive many" (Matt. 24:11).

WOLVES IN SHEEP'S CLOTHING

Look again at Jesus' warning of the counterfeit prophetic ministry that would plague the church:

> Beware of false prophets, who come to you in sheep's clothing, but inwardly they are ravenous wolves. You will know them by their fruits.
>
> —MATTHEW 7:15–16

Jesus said "beware" of false prophets. Why does He warn us so frequently and with such passion? The reason is clear: The counterfeit is very subtle and deceptive. As we saw in the examples in previous chapters, it comes dressed as sheep, not wolves. With appearances so similar it is hard to distinguish the true from the false. Jesus said there would be many, not a few (Matt. 24:11), and that, if possible, even the elect would be deceived by them because of their supernatural gifts. How do we rightly divide between the true and the false? Jesus said their fruit would tell the story. However, we need to understand that fruit includes more than accuracy of their words or their prediction of the future. Let me stress this point: Jesus never said that a true prophet is identified solely by the fact that his words are accurate or came to pass. However, *inaccuracy* is certainly a sign that God was not involved. The Word says:

> And if you say in your heart, "How shall we know the word which the LORD has not spoken?"—when a prophet speaks in the name of the LORD, if the thing does *not* happen or come to pass, that is the thing which the LORD has not spoken; the prophet has spoken it presumptuously; you shall not be afraid of him.
>
> —DEUTERONOMY 18:21–22, EMPHASIS ADDED

God made it clear that if a prophet's words do not come to pass, he is not to be feared or regarded as a prophet. However, this criteria alone is not enough to distinguish the true from the counterfeit, for false prophets can be accurate. The Lord explained that a prophet could speak a word, and it could come to pass, but he is to be rejected if he leads you into idolatry, covetousness, or rebellion (Deut. 13:1–5; Col. 3:5). This man God calls a false prophet because of his fruit. It is a mistake to assume accuracy alone validates an individual as a prophet, yet many—even leaders—make this mistake. We must discern the fruit that remains. Let's look at some examples.

Baalam—a corrupt prophet with a covetous heart—prophesied an accurate word over Israel and predicted the birth of the Messiah. His words are recorded in Scripture. Even though his prophetic words were accurate, his fruit was bad. Jesus said that he "taught Balak to put a stumbling block before the children of Israel, to eat things sacrificed to idols, and to commit sexual immorality" (Rev. 2:14). Baalam was offered substantial wealth if he would curse Israel, but he was not able to curse those God blessed. After this realization he taught Balak how to snare the children of Israel and place them under a curse by enticing them to sin (Num. 31:16; Num. 25:1–9). He did this to retain the reward. His fruit led the people into judgment. Twenty-four thousand Israelites died from the plague that judged their disobedience. Baalam's prophecies were accurate, but his fruit proved to be ungodly. He had mixed the precious with the vile. In Joshua 13:22 he is called a "soothsayer." The children of Israel were commanded to kill him with the edge of the sword in battle. From this we learn that accuracy does not delineate the true from false. Baalam had a genuine gift on his life but corrupted it with the desire for gain. He was a false prophet.

In the New Testament Paul and his companion were "met by a slave girl who had a spirit by which she predicted the future" (Acts 16:16, NIV). She earned a great deal of money for her owners by fortunetelling. It is obvious she was accurate. She was even right on with Paul and his companions, when she cried out, "These men are servants of the Most High God, who are telling you the way to be saved." What she said was accurate, but it was not by the unction of the Holy Spirit but by a spirit of divination. She was accurate but her fruit was bad! Frustrated, Paul cast out the spirit and she was no longer able to predict the future.

Both Baalam and this servant girl were labeled soothsayers, diviners, or false prophets. Both were accurate—one by a genuine gift of God and the other by a spirit of divination. Jesus focused on the motive in Matthew 7:16, because the motive will always reveal itself in the fruit. What is the fruit of a prophet's life and ministry? It is the determining factor. Examine again His words carefully:

> Beware of false prophets, who come to you in sheep's clothing, but inwardly they are ravenous wolves. You will know them by their fruits. Do men gather grapes from thornbushes or figs from thistles? Even so, every good tree bears good fruit, but a bad tree bears bad fruit. A good tree cannot bear bad fruit, nor can a bad tree bear good fruit. Every tree that does not bear good fruit is cut down and thrown into the fire. Therefore by their fruits you will know them.
> —MATTHEW 7:15–20

We've allowed accuracy to cloud our discernment. If you examine the fruit in the modern-day stories in previous chapters, it is easy to see we've embraced words and perhaps prophets whom God would call false.

FRUIT IS SPIRITUALLY DISCERNED

Jesus makes it clear we are to judge prophets by their fruit. Paul and John also said to "test" or "judge" the prophetic (1 Thess. 5:21; 1 John 4:1; 1 Cor. 14:29). This fruit is not discerned by our five natural senses, nor is it identified intellectually—it must be spiritually discerned. Paul wrote, "But he who is spiritual judges all things . . . comparing spiritual things with spiritual" (1 Cor. 2:15, 13). When we repent and purge our hearts of any impure motives and embrace God's truth, then we are in a position to be sensitive to the Holy Spirit's leading. The purpose of this book is to relay more than mere parameters or mental information. I pray it is a vehicle by which the Spirit of God enlightens us that we are trained in righteousness (1 John 2:27).

In Jesus' day there were ministers who "outwardly appear[ed] righteous to men" (Matt. 23:28). Yet inwardly they were full of envy and self-seeking. Their appearances were deceptive until the true motives were made known by the light of God's living Word. Jesus compared their hearts to bad soil that produced evil fruit (Matt. 13:1–23; 15:17–20).

James tells us:

> But if you have bitter jealousy and selfish ambition in your *heart,* do not be arrogant and so lie against the truth. This wisdom is not that which comes down from above, but is earthly, natural, demonic. For where *jealousy* and *selfish ambition* exist, there is disorder and every evil thing.
> —JAMES 3:14–16, NAS, EMPHASIS ADDED

James reveals the atmosphere of their heart as jealous and ambitious. Both are summed up in the term *self-seeking!*

He continues:

> And the *seed* whose fruit is righteousness is sown in peace by those who make peace.
> —JAMES 3:18, NAS, EMPHASIS ADDED

The seeds of jealousy and ambition produce disorder and every evil thing. The seed of peace produces righteousness. Peace is found in contentment, while selfish ambition and jealousy breed within a covetous heart. Again we find the contrast between covetousness and contentment.

James reveals that every form of evil is found in a heart filled with selfish ambition or covetousness. This lends a greater understanding to Paul's words, "Now godliness with contentment is great gain. . . . But those who desire to be rich [covetous—desiring gain] fall into temptation and a snare, and into many foolish and harmful lusts which drown men in destruction and perdition" (1 Tim. 6:6, 9). Notice the use of "fall into." You fall on accident, not on purpose. This again confirms the subtle deception behind covetousness.

A FALSE PROPHET'S MOTIVES

While in prayer, God spoke to my heart this definition of a false prophet in the church, which goes along with what we have seen in Scripture:

> A false prophet is one who comes in My name with his own agenda.

His agenda may be packaged in ministry, but the underlying motive is gain, promotion, or reward. These concealed and hidden motives not only deceive others but the prophet as well. Paul warned, "Impostors will grow worse and worse, deceiving and being deceived" (2 Tim. 3:13). Notice he said it will grow and increase. Over the last decade there has been increase, and the lines are all but blurred between the precious and the vile. We are approaching harvest—not only the reaping of good, but of evil as well. God told me:

> A false prophet will use the gifting I have entrusted to him to carry out his own purposes.

145

It will be used to draw others to themselves and to further their cause, whether it is financial gain, power, recognition, influence, or acceptance. He will deceive himself by distorting Scriptures to fulfill or support his desires.

KNOWN BY FRUIT

Let's discuss some of the more common fruits you find in a false prophet. Bear in mind Jesus' words, "A good tree cannot bear bad fruit, nor can a bad tree bear good fruit." The key word is *bear,* or *produce.* Remember, Jesus said men do not gather grapes from thornbushes or figs from thistles. Why? It is not their nature to produce such fruit. However, you certainly could hang a cluster of grapes on a thornbush, or place a fig among thistles. Likewise, quite often a true word or action may be found among false prophets, but it did not originate with them. This explains God's rebuke through Jeremiah:

> "Therefore behold, I am against the prophets," says the LORD,
> "who steal My words every one from his neighbor."
> —JEREMIAH 23:30

The word was not produced in their mouths nor was it cultivated in their hearts. They stole the words of another, who got it from another, who got it from another and so forth back to its origin—from the mouth of one who truly walked with God. Their words did not come from intimate communion with the Lord bathed in an atmosphere of holy fear (Ps. 25:14).

Another possibility is that they once walked with God and received revelation from Him. Then their hearts grew cold, as in the case of Baalam. Peter confirmed this: "They have forsaken the right way and gone astray, following the way of Balaam" (2 Pet. 2:15). They once knew and walked in the right way, but did not endure Scripture describes those who fall away as "late autumn trees without fruit" (Jude 11–12). Late autumn trees at one time bore fruit, but it is one thing to know truth, and quite another to live it! Truth is not found in the mere repetition of words but in the transformation of hearts. Late autumn trees are no longer in the season of fruit. That season is past and winter is before them. Their leaves drop off as they slip into a dormant sleep. No matter what the case, there is a common denominator of all false prophets: "From the least even to the greatest everyone is given to covetousness" (Jer. 8:10). They are self-seeking. In the following verses Peter described the results of false leaders, which would also apply to false prophets.

> But there were also false prophets among the people, even as there will be false teachers among you, who will secretly bring in destructive heresies, even denying the Lord who bought them, and bring on themselves swift destruction.
> —2 PETER 2:1

The Greek word for *heresies* is *hairesis*. W. E. Vine defines this word as "that which is chosen, and hence, an opinion, especially a self-willed opinion, which is substituted for submission to the power of truth . . ."[1]

False teachers bring in heresies that lead professing believers away from the submission to truth, even to the place of denying the Lord. You may be thinking, *No one could come into our churches today and induce us to deny our Lord Jesus Christ.* You're right— nothing that obvious would succeed today or in Peter's day. Remember, Peter said the teachers would come in secretly or unnoticed. No one could openly confess the denial of Jesus in our churches and go unnoticed. The following verse sheds light on how false ministers do this secretly:

> Everything is pure to those whose hearts are pure. But nothing is pure to those who are *corrupt* and unbelieving, because their minds and consciences are defiled. Such people claim they know God, *but they deny him by the way they live.*
> —TITUS 1:15–16, NLT, EMPHASIS ADDED

To be *corrupt* is to have been polluted. Recall God's word, "For both prophet and priest are polluted" (Jer. 23:11, NAS). From the scripture in Titus we learn it is not their confession, but their way of life that denies the Lord. Jesus said, "By their fruits we will know them," not by what they say—not even if they call Him Lord. For with their mouths they confess the lordship of Jesus, prophesy, and do wonders in His name, yet they are not submitted to His lordship or authority (Matt. 7:15–23). Peter continued:

> And many will follow their destructive ways, because of whom the way of truth will be blasphemed. By covetousness they will *exploit* you with deceptive words.
> —2 PETER 2:2–3, EMPHASIS ADDED

Again we uncover the motive "covetousness." *Exploit* means "to abuse, profit by, or take advantage of." Therefore false ministers take advantage of others by way of deceptive, smooth words. It may sound like God's voice, but it is not His motives. Through deception and covetousness they take advantage of the young, simple, or wounded.

A Heart Trained in Covetousness

Peter goes on to say they have "a heart trained in covetous practices" (2 Pet. 2:14). When you are trained in something, you can do it without thinking. It becomes second nature. When we first learned to tie our shoes it was awkward and required our focused attention. Now we do it without thinking. We are trained. With someone trained in covetousness the same is true.

I know of a man who worked for a minister who exploited people through direct mail. Consultants (or in this case experts in greed) came in and mixed the precious with the vile. They exaggerated and stretched stories to elicit funds. Their letters played off the anointing on the minister and promised answers to prayers or religious trinkets in exchange for offerings. At first employees and even the man's wife questioned their leader's decision. I think even the leader's conscience was pricked in the beginning. But enough Scriptures were quoted out of context until all consciences were silenced. Money poured in as never before. Obviously God was blessing and leading them. Salaries and bonuses grew until they eventually were trained in covetousness. Now they exploited God's Word and therefore His people without a second thought!

This is happening today in abundance. Many a marketing company is happy to help ministries come up with clever ways to get money. Twisted Scriptures hide covetous desires. Direct mail arrives at your door proclaiming wants as needs. These letters transfer guilt on their recipients that if they don't respond, the will of God will not be accomplished. They will lose their jubilee or one-hundred-fold return! I am not talking about valid relief efforts to the hurting and hungry but of those trained in greed. Paul prophetically glimpsed this and wrote, "They will act as if they are religious, but they will reject the power that could make them godly. You must stay away from people like that. They are the kind who work their way into people's homes and win the confidence of vulnerable women . . . " (2 Tim. 3:5–6, NLT). But today it is not only the women who are vulnerable.

Then there is the misuse of the broadcast media. Many telethons are conducted in a godly way. They alert and update God's people to the genuine needs of the ministry and allow others the opportunity to partner in their outreach. Alongside this is the abuse of telethons. Many will bring in the experts (ministers) who have proven track records in the area of fund raising. I've watched them promise blessings for all who give, while you are left with the impression that those who don't respond would not be blessed. There is a lot of excitement and sometimes favors extended whenever someone responds with a large gift. Micah warned:

> This is what the LORD says to you false prophets: "You are leading my people astray! You promise peace for those who give you food."
>
> —MICAH 3:5, NLT

One telethon in America recently had a prophetic minister who gave personal prophecies to all who pledged a designated amount of money (it exceeded one thousand dollars). The really sad part is that many responded after the promise of a personal word. What about those who could not give that much? Are they deprived of

God's direction because they can't afford it? Who ever bought a word, healing, or deliverance from Jesus? What about the widow who gave two mites? Jesus sat opposite the treasury and watched as people put their money into the treasury. Many of the rich put in large sums. Why then was a poor widow who threw in two mites singled out? Jesus called His disciples to Himself and shared why: "Assuredly, I say to you that this poor widow has put in more than all those who have given to the treasury; for they all put in out of their abundance, but she out of her poverty put in all that she had, her whole livelihood" (Mark 12:41–44). Jesus paid attention to the one who gave the least in the eyes of man knowing it to be the most in the eyes of God. In this telethon those who gave the most received the attention or the prophecy. Hear what Micah said:

> Her leaders judge for a bribe, her priests teach for a price, and her prophets tell fortunes for money. Yet they lean upon the LORD and say, "Is not the LORD among us? No disaster will come upon us."
>
> —MICAH 3:11, NIV

We keep proclaiming that God is with us, that He is in the middle of the projects designed to get money from God's people. But is He? We have mistaken financial success as a sign of His involvement. That is erroneous. In the Old Testament false prophets lived in luxury while the true ones roamed the wilderness. False prophets were honored in their lifetime while true ones were often only honored after their deaths.

PROPHESYING FOR MONEY

Notice Micah said prophets tell fortunes for money. Today this runs rampant. One prophet charges hundreds of dollars to prepare a personal word for you for the next twelve months. Others will impart ministry gifts for an offering. One national prophetic conference in their advertisement promised that each *registrant* would receive prophetic ministry, activation, and impartation of prophetic gifts. Sounds spiritual and appealing. But the previous line had stated the required registration fee. So if I pay my registration fee I will receive the impartation and activation of my prophetic gifts! What about the Holy Spirit's leading? What if God doesn't want these precious gifts bought and sold so cheaply? Money is cheap compared to the laying down of your life. I thought gifts were given by the Lord as He wills. To some they are not gifts; they are purchases. Have we become those who peddle the Word of God for profit and merchandise His gifts? I would like to tell you this was an obscure meeting, but every one of the ministers involved in the conference is known nationally. Have we ministers traded in our discernment for involvement with those trained in covetousness?

I am not saying it is wrong to charge a registration fee. Anyone who holds a conference incurs expenses that can be covered by those who attend. What I take exception to is the implication and promise of spiritual impartation in exchange for money. It is wrong to draw people by promising them a personal word. This lures people into unscriptural practices even if the motive is simply to cover the expenses of the conference. Registration fees in themselves are not disturbing. It is the manipulation of people by promising a personal word for all paying participants.

Whatever happened to believing God for the finances? Is His arm too short that He cannot provide for what He commands us to do? Yes, God's promises are true, and we receive a harvest when we give or sow, but that must not be our motivation for giving or sowing. We cannot outgive Him (Mark 10:29–30). If Jesus followed the pattern of today He would have told the rich young ruler to sell all he had and give it to His ministry, not the poor! Then He would have said, "Hey, man, don't walk away. Don't you realize if you give to Me, you'll get a hundredfold return! This is your jubilee!" No, Jesus never used the benefits of obedience to entice people to follow Him, even though He is our jubilee.

I believe we do have a heavenly account, and that account increases as we give. But hear Paul's heart: "Not that I seek the gift, but I seek the fruit that abounds to your account" (Phil. 4:17). This is the heart of a true prophet. In contrast, the false prophet will place his wants before the needs of those to whom he ministers.

False prophets crave the titles and recognition of man. True prophets never did. Watch John the Baptist's response when questioned by the priests and Levites as to his true identity and position. When asked if he were the Christ he answered that he was not. Then "they asked him, 'What then? Are you Elijah?' He said, 'I am not.' 'Are you the Prophet?' And he answered, 'No'" (John 1:21). Why didn't he reveal that he was the Elijah prophet as the angel Gabriel and Jesus both said he was (Luke 1:17; Matt. 17:12–13)? I believe he was not willing to be labeled or to play along with their political game.

These men were into titles, positions, and popularity. They craved the praise and recognition of men. They had not come out to humble themselves through baptism but to check John out. Their ears could not hear his message of repentance because they were veiled in religious self-righteousness and pride. They came out of curiosity and envy. Who was this renegade who threatened their status quo? Who had given him authority? Could he be brought under their control? John saw through this and called them *snakes!* He saw through their religious masks and viewed their motives.

John finally described his identity this way: "I am 'the voice of one crying in the wilderness: "Make straight the way of the LORD""" (John 1:22). He diverted the focus from himself and directed it to the Lord. He longed to see these captive religious leaders freed from the bondage of titles and the fear of man. He wanted them to turn back to God. He chose the words he spoke with great care, careful not to mix his opinions or agenda in with the Lord's.

In days of old, prophets would not change the message to please the people. As a result, when they came to town the elders feared.

> So Samuel did what the LORD said, and went to Bethlehem.
> And the elders of the town trembled at his coming, and said,
> "Do you come peaceably?"
> —1 SAMUEL 16:4

First, notice that Samuel came in obedience to the Lord. He was afraid Saul would hear and have him killed, but he went. This obedience created an atmosphere of godly fear. The godly trembled as he approached. But today's prophetic seminars are attended with excitement, as though attending a fortunetelling event.

If God has placed you in the ministry of a prophet, you will not have to put your title or spiritual office under your picture. He will make it known through the fruit of His words, as He did with Samuel, one of the greatest Old Testament prophets.

> So Samuel grew, and the LORD was with him and let none of his words fall to the ground. And all Israel from Dan to Beersheba knew that Samuel had been established as a prophet of the LORD.
>
> —1 SAMUEL 3:19–20

Your fruit reveals your call just as fruit reveals the type of tree.

Fruit is what proceeds from the heart of a person and is spiritually discerned. Not all ministers who bear the title of bishop, doctor, apostle, prophet, pastor, and so on are covetous and desirous of the praise of man. With many the title is a product of their religious affiliations or denominations and holds little meaning. A label or title does not mean wickedness of heart any more than the absence of one means a pure one. The fruit determines whether they minister out of love for God and His people.

THE TARGET OF FALSE PROPHETS

Jesus compared false prophets to wolves in sheep's clothing. Let's briefly discuss wolves. I enjoy learning about wildlife behavior and have enjoyed documentaries of this animal. Though my knowledge is limited, their method of hunting is to isolate their prey from the herd. By singling them out they cut off any protection the flock can offer. Then they attack, first crippling, then devouring the prey. Solomon warned:

> A man who isolates himself seeks his own desire; he rages against all wise judgment.
>
> —PROVERBS 18:1

Isolation separates a believer from the direction and protection of the shepherd. Without the shelter of the body, they are easy prey. Remember how Paul fervently warned the elders:

> For I know this, that after my departure savage wolves will come in among you, not sparing the flock. Also from among yourselves men will rise up, speaking perverse things, to draw away the disciples after themselves.
>
> —ACTS 20:29–30

The most easily isolated or singled out are the weak, the young, or the wounded. These are the ones most susceptible to counterfeit prophecy. The young are easily isolated because they are not mature and skilled in the Word of God. They have yet to develop discernment. As a church we must protect them. Jesus charged Peter to feed and tend or protect both His *lambs* and His sheep (John 21:15–16). This is the responsibility of the true shepherd. The pure word of God guards young believers and protects them from the entrapment of the false words. New converts of the early church "were continually devoting themselves to the apostles' teaching and to fellowship, to the breaking of bread and to prayer" (Acts 2:42, NAS).

Weak sheep are also easily isolated because they lack the strength of the Word of Righteousness (Heb. 5:13). To counteract this we are admonished, "Now we who are strong ought to bear the weaknesses of those without strength and not just please ourselves" (Rom. 15:1, NAS).

I have found, however, the number one target of the false prophetic is the wounded or offended. They are the most vulnerable because *offended people isolate themselves.* Proverbs 18:19 tells us: "A brother offended is harder to win than a strong city." Strong cities had walls around them. The walls protected them and kept out the unwanted and those who are indebted to them. Likewise offended persons build walls of protection around their hearts. They can sit among a congregation of thousands, yet be alone. They may be members of large families, yet they are isolated in their hearts. They pull away to protect themselves, never guessing they become more vulnerable to the deception of false prophets.

Jesus foresaw this in the last days:

> And then many will be offended, will betray one another, and will hate one another. Then many false prophets will rise up and deceive many.
>
> —MATTHEW 24:10–11

The *many* that the *many* false prophets deceive are the *many* who are offended. An offense leaves one susceptible to divination. Often they use words that accurately rehearse past hurts and pain while flattering them in their offense. This blinds their discernment and perpetuates an inward focus. These words do not encourage them to forgive and take up the cross, which signifies self-denial. During this type of word the offended person briefly lets down a portion of the wall long enough to embrace whatever is said. The person will pull away from anyone who does not support the word and draw close to the one who gave it. Often they pull away from pastors and friends.

SUMMARY

I have only touched on this subject, but I want to reiterate the most important difference between a true and false prophet:

> A false prophet uses his God-entrusted gifts to draw others to himself. A true prophet draws them to the heart of God.

When you leave the meeting of a true prophet you should feel an intense desire to seek God. His words will either point you back to Jesus or sharpen your present focus. There will be a new clarity. In contrast, when you leave the meeting of a false prophet you'll find yourself wanting to go back for another word any time you need encouragement or direction! There is a danger when we embrace another mediator outside of Christ. He rent the veil so that man could come into the presence of the Father. There in His presence is where you will find the fulfillment of every need and deepest desire.

The love of truth sharpens
our discernment and keeps us
error free.

14

THE LOVE OF
THE TRUTH

When Jesus warned, "See to it that no one misleads you," He communicated that *it is our responsibility to guard against deception* (Matt. 24:4, NAS). This warning has little value unless we realize and establish in our minds that the path of truth is never easy. In fact, we are promised it will be accompanied by hardship (Mark 4:17). Tribulation and suffering are traveling companions on the road of obedience. Those prone to comfort and ease will find themselves veering toward the path of "the good life," especially when directions to it are handed out as "words from the Lord."

WE ARE RESPONSIBLE

An excellent example of a false word of comfort is found in 1 Kings 13. God sent a prophet to Bethel to confront the wicked king Jeroboam. God gave the messenger very specific instructions: He was not to eat, drink, or return the way he came. He obeyed and boldly delivered God's message with power and authority. The king became furious and stretched out his hand to arrest this man of God, and it withered. The king then pleaded for the prophet to intercede to the Lord on his behalf. The man of God prayed, and the king's hand was restored to normal again.

157

A grateful though unrepentant Jeroboam invited the prophet to join him at his palace to be refreshed and rewarded. Without hesitation the prophet refused the king's invitation, and repeated his divine instructions: "It was commanded me by the word of the LORD, saying, 'You shall not eat bread, nor drink water, nor return by the same way you came'" (1 Kings 13:9). In obedience he immediately departed on a different route back to his home in Judah.

Word of this spread quickly, and an old prophet dwelling in Bethel pursued this young prophet. He found him sitting under an oak tree resting. His journey had been long, and the confrontation was intense. He was hungry, thirsty, and weak, which meant he was vulnerable! It is in this setting of hardship and discomfort that deception seeks to strikes!

The old prophet invited him back for refreshment and fellowship. Again the man of God repeated his instruction: "I cannot return with you nor go in with you; neither can I eat bread nor drink water with you in this place. For I have been told by the word of the LORD, 'You shall not eat bread nor drink water there, nor return by going the way you came'" (1 Kings 13:16–17).

The old prophet quickly answered, "'I too am a prophet as you are, and an angel spoke to me by the word of the LORD saying, 'Bring him back with you to your house, that he may eat bread and drink water'" (1 Kings 13:18). God must have seen he was tired and changed His mind. Maybe it was enough that he refused the king. Perhaps God didn't mean what He had said. No, the Scriptures explain, "He [the old prophet] was lying to him."

It is important to note that God hates it when His name is used to lend authority to our own agendas. He bluntly says so through the prophet Jeremiah:

> But stop using this phrase, "prophecy from the LORD." For people are using it to give authority to their own ideas, turning upside down the words of our God, the living God, the LORD Almighty.
>
> —JEREMIAH 23:36, NLT

God says when people use His name to carry out their own ideas that it turns "upside down the words of our God." It brings in confusion, doubt, and reasoning. This causes us to lean unto our own understanding and leave the straight path.

IT WASN'T THE OBVIOUS THAT DECEIVED

This young man of God left the straight path, which brought discomfort, to follow the old prophet to a place of comfort. At the time and in his condition, the lie looked more reasonable than God's truth. But this temporary comfort came at a high price. As they ate, the word of the Lord came to the old prophet:

> Thus says the LORD: "Because you have disobeyed the word of the LORD, and have not kept the commandment which the LORD your God commanded you, but you came back, ate bread, and drank water in the place of which the LORD said to you, 'Eat no bread and drink no water,' your corpse shall not come to the tomb of your fathers."
>
> —1 KINGS 13:21–22

Within hours of giving the deceptive word the old prophet spoke a true message from heaven. Again, as we saw with Baalam, a corrupt prophet can have the genuine gift of prophesy operating in his life. The disobedient young prophet left the old prophet's house, was mauled by a lion and dead within hours, thus fulfilling the word of the Lord!

Even though a sumptuous reward banquet at the palace was more inviting than bread and water at the prophet's house, this young prophet had no problem turning down the king. It didn't require a lot of discernment to see through the king's offer. But when a fellow prophet or believer came with a word that offered comfort to this weary young prophet, he was taken in. He thought this was God's blessing for his obedience. Little did he know that he would soon bear the consequences of this choice, even though he acted on good faith when the old prophet lied!

Has God changed the way He looks at things today? Or have we modified our view to fit our frailties? It doesn't take a lot of

159

discernment to recognize and avoid wicked leaders or those in blatant error. These are wolves in wolf skin. It is the subtler form that confuses us—the wolves in sheep's clothing who bring smooth words and have spiritual gifts. I have spoken to pastors of congregations that have been stung by polluted ministry. They are bewildered as they question, "John, they did do some good, and I know there is a genuine gift working through them. How then could so much devastation come out of them? How is the good so entangled with the bad?" When I ask them what the overall fruit of the meetings was, they are quick to admit the overall fruit of the meetings was confusion and destruction.

We cannot open ourselves up and embrace just any word from any person. We must realize our responsibility to discern the true from the false. Those in leadership will give an account for those entrusted to their care who have been plundered or defiled by the false words to which they have subjected them and have not confronted. God has made a way to identify and escape the lies and deceptions.

THE LOVE OF THE TRUTH

Paul explained that the reason so many are easily misled in these latter days is because they "did not receive the love of the truth" (2 Thess. 2:10). The love of truth sharpens our discernment and keeps us error free. Those who have developed this love of truth will never elevate a gift (such as prophecy) above God's wisdom. The love of truth always chooses to submit to obedience even when they cannot see any personal benefit from it. This guards against any comfortable lies or deceptions tagged with "thus saith the Lord."

In the incident of the young man of God and older prophet we find a key to this lack of discernment. When offered a "word" that would relieve his hardship, he repeated his instructions, "I *cannot* return with you nor go in with you; neither can I eat bread nor drink water with you in this place. For I have been told by the word of the LORD, 'You shall not eat bread nor drink water there, nor return by going the way you came'" (1 Kings 13:16–17, emphasis added). However, hidden in this response is his will. We find it in the word *cannot.* Difficulty and discomfort had set in, the task was almost done, and his enthusiasm was waning. The word of the Lord was no longer directing and fulfilling him. It is restraining him.

Let's contrast *cannot* with the words of David. He says, "I delight to do Your will, O my God, and Your law is within my heart" (Ps. 40:8). And again in Psalm 119:47, "I will delight myself in Your commandments, which I love." David loved truth even when those closest to him tried to dissuade him. His love for the truth blocked any inroad of deception from his heart.

An example of this is found as David hid in the desert skirting the wrath of Saul. David had already proved his innocence before the king. (See 1 Samuel 24.) Yet again Saul and three thousand soldiers pursued him to the wilderness of Ziph. It was clear to David that Saul is determined to kill him.

One evening David and Abishai slipped into Saul's camp. No guards saw them because God had placed the entire camp into a deep sleep. They wove through the army of sleeping men until they stood over the sleeping Saul.

Abishai pleaded with David, "God has delivered your enemy into your hand this day. Now therefore, please, let me strike him at once with the spear, right to the earth; and I will not have to strike him a second time!" (1 Sam. 26:8).

Abishai had many good reasons why David should order him to strike Saul. First and foremost, Saul had murdered eighty-five innocent priests, their wives, and children—in cold blood! The nation was in danger under the leadership of such a mad man.

Second, God had anointed David the next king of Israel by the word of Samuel. It was time David claimed his inheritance! Did he want to end up a dead man and never fulfill the prophecy?

Third, wasn't Saul out with an army of three thousand to kill David and his men? Now was the time to kill or be killed. Surely this was self-defense. Abishai knew any court of law would uphold their actions.

Fourth, wasn't it God who had put this army into a sleep so deep that they could walk right up to Saul? This was a God-given chance, and it might never come again. Now was the time to seize the fulfillment of the word!

Although these reasons sounded good, made sense, and were presented by the mouth of an encouraging brother, they were in fact a test for David. All of Abishai's arguments were true, but they were not *truth*. God tested David to see how he would respond. What manner of king would he be? Would he exercise his authority to serve others or himself? Would he act as judge or give place to God's righteous judgment? David knew Saul was not his servant to judge. If David coveted the throne in the least, he would have ordered Saul killed. As David looked at the dim outline of Saul he saw something else. We see it in his response:

> Do not destroy him; for who can stretch out his hand against the LORD's anointed, and be guiltless? The LORD forbid that I should stretch out my hand against the LORD's anointed.
> —1 SAMUEL 26:9–11

David saw the Lord's hand between him and Saul. His love for God's truth restrained him from taking by force what God had promised him, though killing Saul would have put an end to his uncomfortable state. Though a fugitive, he was free from the covetousness that tormented Saul. He wanted truth exalted over his own well-being. This pursuit of well-being cost the young prophet his life to deception. He turned from God's word to the reasoning of the counterfeit.

If we are to walk free from deception we must allow the Holy Spirit to develop a consuming love for truth deep within us. How does one arrive at such a place? It is found in trusting the faithfulness of God. David wrote:

> Trust in the LORD, and do good; dwell in the land, and feed on His faithfulness. Delight yourself also in the LORD, and He shall give you the desires of your heart. Commit your way to the LORD, trust also in Him, and He shall bring it to pass. He shall bring forth your righteousness as the light, and your justice as the noonday. Rest in the LORD, and wait patiently for Him.
> —PSALM 37:3–7

David instructs us to "feed on His faithfulness" as we wait for His promises to come forth. There have been times when reciting the promises no longer fed my soul. Adversity drew near while the answers drifted beyond my reach. In these times I encouraged myself in the Lord. I trusted His faithfulness, knowing He would bring forth His righteous word. During the uncomfortable waiting process I was approached and offered a way out of my discomfort, but deep within I knew it wasn't God's way.

God promises to grant us the desires of our heart, according to the Psalms. Many of us are guilty of misapplying this scripture. We view it as a word to fulfill our covetous desires. But this is not what David was saying. David exhorted us to delight ourselves in Him and commit our ways to Him, because God in return places righteous desires in us and brings them to pass. By examining the lives of those who walked closely with the Lord in the New Testament we discover their greatest desire was to know God intimately and to see others walk with Him.

Paul expressed it this way: "My heart's desire and prayer to God for Israel is that they may be saved" (Rom. 10:1). Do you hear his desire? It was not for personal gain, comfort, or recognition. Rather it was God's passion for Israel's salvation that burned in him. In fact, he forsook his own rights and privileges for the sake of not seeing his desire hindered. Hear his heart as he writes, "We would rather put up with anything than put an obstacle in the way of the Good News about Christ" (1 Cor. 9:12, NLT). It would be difficult to deceive such a man. May God help us all!

John the Apostle was another. He wrote, "I have no greater joy than to hear that my children walk in truth" (3 John 4). He echoed Paul's greatest desire. Others in the New Testament had the same attitude. We find nothing in their voiced desires of their own comfort, success, or even financial prosperity.

Paul described our day as difficult or perilous because the love of self, money, and pleasure would overshadow the love of truth. Hearts would stray far from the motives of David, Paul, or John. Because of this they would be "always learning and never able to come to the knowledge of the truth" (2 Tim. 3:1–7). Though they may travel from churches to conferences to campmeetings to seminars, they remain unchanged. They gather information without transformation. Information is not knowledge. Knowledge comes through hunger, humility, and application. God reserves knowledge for those who love it.

Religion can be zealous and passionate. The Pharisees were passionate enough to kill for what they believed. But you can love doctrine or religion and yet not love truth. The truth is not a teaching; it is only found in the person of Jesus. He promised, "I am the way, *the truth,* and the light" (John 14:6, emphasis added).

Those who love truth will love Jesus. They embrace and obey God's Word even to what may appear to be their own hurt. They desire the fulfillment of God's Word not because they love self but because they love God. Their greatest desire is to see others in the will and presence of God. They would willingly suffer in obedience to God's whole counsel than cling to a word promising personal success or comfort at the expense of truth. They take up the cross and lay down their lives.

This type of submission exhibits true humility. Humility is not oppressive or restrictive but an agreement with truth. We find it when we lay down our agenda, desires, and will and become impassioned to fulfill God's. Though this is not easy, the humble are empowered by God's grace, and His grace is more than sufficient to keep us from deception (1 Pet. 5:5)!

If we hear words in our mind or are given words from another without a witness of peace, the word should be rejected. The witness of peace is the umpire or decision maker.

15

TESTING AND HANDLING
PERSONAL PROPHECY

Today many are encouraged to go and get a word from a prophet. This idea originates from the Old Testament practice of consulting a prophet for direction. But are we still under the Old Testament? Does God only speak through prophets? No, God clearly states:

> In the past God spoke to our forefathers through the prophets at many times and in various ways, but in these last days he has spoken to us by his Son.
>
> —HEBREWS 1:1–2, NIV

The Spirit of God did not dwell in the Jew of the Old Testament as He does within every believer today. Before the sacrifice of Christ, He was only upon select individuals, usually prophets or priests. Therefore the forefathers, in order to inquire of the Lord, would have to go to either a prophet or a priest. It is not so in the New Testament. Jesus said of the Holy Spirit who would be given to each believer:

> He dwells with you and will be in you . . . He will guide you into all truth; for He will not speak on His own authority, but whatever He hears He will speak; and He will tell you things to come.
>
> —JOHN 14:17; 16:13

167

He takes the things of Christ and reveals them to us. He comes not in His own authority but in Christ's and speaks the words of Jesus, not His own. This repeats the pattern of Jesus and the Father. Jesus came as the Word of God, and the Holy Spirit comes as the Word of the Son. There is no other mediator through which we would inquire of the Lord. Jesus outlined this new and living way for His disciples:

> Most assuredly, I say to you, whatever you ask the Father in My name He will give you. Until now you have asked nothing in My name. Ask, and you will receive, that your joy may be full.
> —JOHN 16:23–24

James also confirms our ability to directly inquire:

> If any of you lacks wisdom, let him ask of God, who gives to all liberally and without reproach, and it will be given to him.
> —JAMES 1:5

Notice James did not say, "Let him seek a prophet to ask of God." Prophetic mediators are not found in the New Testament. Jesus is our mediator (1 Tim. 2:5). If we need to inquire, we approach the Father in Jesus' name. Old Testament saints did not have this privilege.

If God has a word He wants to get to us, He will at times use a prophetic messenger, but we are not to seek a prophet. We are to seek the Lord. I have learned of two different scenarios in which God sends a messenger. Though there may be others, these are most common. First, if for some reason we cannot hear what He is speaking directly to us, He may speak through another. Often this may be due to hearts that have hardened through disobedience. In this case God sends a messenger to call us to obedience.

The second case in which God will speak to us through another is when intense tribulation or persecution lies ahead. He will arm us with a strengthening word that we might fight effectively (1 Tim. 1:18).

STANDARDS FOR JUDGING

The Scriptures tell us we are judge both prophecy (1 Cor. 14:29; 1 Thess. 5:20–21) and the spirit of the one delivering it (1 John 4:1) before receiving it. How is this done? A formula would be restrictive and possibly damaging. As you've read the examples in this book coupled with the Word of God, this equipping has begun. However, there are a few key truths to be considered when judging a word.

First, let's strip away a fallacy we've used to judge them in the past: Prophecy confirms what is in your heart. This is not always true. Ahab heard what he wanted to hear from four hundred prophets of Israel. They prophesied success against the Syrians and confirmed his battle plans. But we learned this word was given according to the idolatry of his heart. This idolatry lured him to his death.

Let's look at the New Testament. Jesus told Peter he would deny Him three times before the rooster crowed. Not only did this not confirm what was in Peter's heart, he argued and boldly declared that he would die first! Though Peter did not accept this word from Jesus it came to pass.

Another widely accepted misconception: If you're not sure about a word, put it on the shelf, and if it is God it will come to pass. Setting something on a shelf is not dealing with the spiritual forces behind the word. If it is false, it will hinder us. Pollution and defilement will set in. The Word of God tells us to judge, not shelf it!

THE WRITTEN WORD OF GOD

Our first and foremost standard for judging any word is that is must not contradict the Word of God. It is interesting to note a final word of warning in the Bible:

> And I solemnly declare to everyone who hears the prophetic words of this book: If anyone adds anything to what is written here, God will add to that person the plagues described in this book. And if anyone removes any of the words of this

prophetic book, God will remove that person's share in the tree of life and in the holy city that are described in this book.
—REVELATION 22:18–19, NLT

I believe this not only applies to the Book of Revelation but to all scripture, for the Bible is a prophetic book. Revelation is God's final chapter of all biblical writings, and He wanted this warning made firm at the end. I do not believe it is coincidental this warning occurs in this location of the Bible. Proverbs reiterates:

Every word of God is pure; He is a shield to those who put their trust in Him. Do not add to His words, lest He rebuke you, and you be found a liar.
—PROVERBS 30:5–6

In this book I have tried my best to back each thought and example with the written Word of God. Even though many examples of the prophetic words do not contradict chapter and verse, they still should be judged in light of God's written Word.

THE WITNESS OF THE HOLY SPIRIT

Our second safeguard is the inward witness of the Holy Spirit. In some cases this may be the only resource we have, such as when the prophetic messages cannot be confirmed by the written Word of God. Paul tells us, "For as many as are led by the Spirit of God, these are sons of God" (Rom. 8:14). Notice we are to be led by the Spirit of God, not by prophecy! Prophecy is to be subject to and judged by the Spirit of God. Paul tell us the preeminent way the Holy Spirit leads: "The Spirit Himself bears witness with our spirit . . . " (Rom. 8:16).

Notice He bears witness with our *spirit.* This raises two important points. First, this witness is not in our heads but in our hearts. Second, His witness is not found in words but with peace, or the lack of it. Paul expounds in his letter to another church:

And let the peace (soul harmony which comes) from Christ

rule (act as umpire continually) in your hearts [deciding and settling with finality all questions that arise in your minds.]
—COLOSSIANS 3:15, AMP

It does not matter if this word comes from another or if we've heard it within our hearts, the witness of peace found through the Spirit of Christ is to be the umpire at all times. If we sense peace in our hearts it is the Holy Spirit's confirmation of truth. If there is unrest or grieving in our hearts, it is not the Spirit of God who has spoken.

This cannot be overstressed. We must settle this fact firmly in our minds. If we hear words in our mind or are given words from another without a witness of peace, the word should be rejected. The witness of peace is the umpire or decision maker.

When we needed an administrator for our ministry operations I searched for over a year for the right person. During this time four good men were suggested. We reviewed resumés and interviewed two of them. Three of them had qualifications beyond my dreams. One had military awards as an administrator; another administrated a company from a small beginning to a large corporation in a few years; the last had more than twenty years of experience as administrator of a well-known and respected international ministry.

Regardless of their glowing accomplishments, there was little or no peace in our hearts. Friends questioned me while my own intellect screamed. I thought, *Have you become so religious that you can't even hire a good man when you see one?* With each turn down I thought, *Am I ever going to get the help we need?* With the third person I talked myself into moving ahead. Yet deep in my heart there was no peace. This unrest or check became so strong I finally realized hiring this person was definitely not God, and God was merciful.

During the course of this my wife would say, "Before you hire anyone, you ought to talk with Scott." Scott had helped us a few times on a volunteer basis. After all the others, I asked him if he would be interested. He prayed and said he was. The day he met with us in my office, God's peace and presence flooded my wife and my hearts as well as the entire atmosphere of the office. We kept glancing at each other during the interview in amazement. We were shocked to sense such peace when every time before there had been nothing but unrest. We knew beyond a doubt this was God's choice because the Holy Spirit bore witness with it. Scott is a great blessing to the ministry team. All the other men were very godly, but just not God's choice for that position.

PEACE, NOT ACCURACY, IS THE UMPIRE

Over the years I've been given so many words that I can't recall them all. However, only a few were truly God's words. Those few I remember as though they were yesterday. When God speaks, you don't forget it! There was one common denominator in all these true words: In each I sensed the presence of God, and there was a witness of peace in my heart. Even the words that brought conviction and correction to my life were accompanied deep within by this witness of peace.

My first year as a youth pastor in the 1980s I experienced much favor and success. After being in my position for a year, a visiting pastor whom I knew and respected said, "John, God gave me a word for you. He told me you are about to go through a death process, and He is going to use this church to bring it forth. It will be tough, but you will come out of it walking closer to the Lord and with greater authority on your ministry."

He couldn't have derived this message from any natural information. I had just participated in a church service where I had shared with the congregation about a very powerful missions trip from which we'd just returned with fifty-six of our youth. I had even given a report on our youth television program. Things were great, and I was on a high. This word did not correlate with the last twelve months. However, even as he spoke I sensed a strong witness in my heart. There was a peace—certainly no emotional excitement—but a knowing that this was God.

Over the next few months it seemed all hell broke loose against me. Adversity arose all around me. Some was due to my immaturity, but most had nothing to do with anything I had done. The most difficult trial came from a man who did not like me or the message I preached to the youth. Normally this wouldn't bother me, but he was in a position of authority over me. God had me bring a strong word of purity and repentance to the young people, and his son was in the youth group.

Conviction stirred in his son's heart. He came to us distraught that the lifestyle he saw at home fell short of how he was challenged to live. This and other personality conflicts made his father determined to get rid of me. He would go to the head pastor and stir his anger against me with false accusations. Then he would turn around and tell me that the senior pastor was against me but that he was standing up for me. He would smile to my face, though he intended to destroy me.

It escalated for several months until he convinced the senior pastor to fire me. On the day I was to be released, the senior pastor changed his mind. A few months later when I was out of town, all the wrong this man had done was exposed, and he was the one let go. This and a number of other incidents made it a year of refining such as I had never known before.

I remembered how that word gave me strength during the very difficult times. I encouraged myself in it, and by it waged warfare on the discouragement and despair that raged against my mind. Several times I reminded myself that God had seen this coming, and in all the hardship there was a promise of drawing closer to Him. Right from the beginning, I knew from the inward witness this was a true prophetic word for me. In review, that year forged a lot of character growth, more than I had experienced before. Just as the word had said, out of the trial came a closer walk with Jesus and His godly wisdom and strength.

On the other hand, I have been given words that were amazingly accurate about my past and present yet carried no witness of God's presence or peace. An incident that happened years ago stands out. I was called out in a prophetic meeting. This man had never seen me, yet he spoke with great accuracy about my past and present. As he spoke I thought, *This is amazingly accurate, but why don't I feel the presence or witness of God?* What he said was so exciting and what I wanted to hear, so I suppressed this lack of the witness in my heart.

I accepted his words based on their accuracy. As a result I began to view everything from that point forth filtered through what he had said. This caused my wife and I a lot of unrest. A few years passed, and one of the pivotal points he said would definitely happen did not. In fact, the opposite came true. It was something we had no control over, and it opened our eyes to how fruitless we had been. We had been in limbo, looking at everything from the wrong perspective of his words.

Before I understood the truths in this book I was vulnerable to words that were accurate yet lacked the witness of the Spirit of God. I allowed them to incorrectly affect my outlook and expectations of the future. Since God revealed what I've shared in this book, it has been easier to recognize when He is truly speaking. It is my prayer this book will bring this clarity to you.

HOW TO HANDLE FALSE PROPHECY

You may be asking, *What do I do if I've received a word I know is not from God?* If the word comes from a fellow believer who is not a leader over you, it is best to stop it as soon as you know it is a counterfeit word. A number of years ago I was with several Christian couples at a home. Toward the end of the evening we started praying, and a woman in the group began giving words. When she came over to me I had no peace and sensed no presence or witness of the Spirit. In fact, I was alarmed and sensed something was wrong. Before the end of the first sentence I knew it was not God. I interrupted, "Please stop." She stopped, surprised by my interruption. I gently but firmly said, "What you're saying is not from the Spirit of God but from your own inspiration."

It was uncomfortable, not only for her and I, but for the other couples as well. She left soon afterward. Other couples thanked me, because she was in the habit of doing this with people and probably would have gone through the whole group. She used these words to control her pastor and some of his elders. When he broke free from her control she left and started her own church.

What if the word comes from a leader? The Bible says we are not to rebuke an elder. When I first started traveling, I sensed an alarm when I was being introduced by the pastor of the church. Then the pastor said, "John, God has given me a word for you." To confront this pastor the way I had confronted the woman would have been out of order. Inside I put up a wall in my heart, and said within myself, *I do not accept this as from God, and this word will not penetrate my heart.*

The pastor walked up to me to deliver the word, but then just stared at me with a dumbfounded look, then turned around and said nothing. The following day the pastor told me, "Last night I had a word for you, but when I walked up and looked at you it left me. I found myself with nothing to say." I told the pastor that I believed if the word had been from God it wouldn't have left so easily.

More often than not there is not a sudden and strong sense of alarm. In these cases I usually listen to the word while looking within for the Holy Spirit's witness. I always pray within myself, "Holy Spirit, show me if this is of You." If I do not sense a witness, I handle it the following way.

If it is a word of peace and prosperity that I know is not from the Holy Spirit, I simply tell the person I don't believe it is God's word. If they persist and try to convince me that God has shown them this, then I bluntly tell them I do not receive their words. I reject these words in order to block defilement.

If it is a word of correction, I handle it differently. The validity of correction is not always easy to discern. If any pride is in your heart it can overshadow the witness of the Spirit. This happened when Jesus gave Peter the words predicting his denial. Rebukes and correction should be carefully considered and prayed about.

I have also found people can deliver correct messages with the wrong motive or attitude. It is hard to test whether it is the word or the motive that sets off the alarm. Yet if there is truth to what they say I should take it to prayer and remain open to what God speaks to my heart. Jesus said, "Agree with your adversary quickly" (Matt. 5:25). Your agreement to pray about it does not mean you have necessarily received their words but that your heart is open to God's direction. I have found a few of these words have resulted in effective correction, which has produced godly humility and character in my life.

BREAKING THE POWER BEHIND WORDS

I have learned that quite often counterfeit words carry spiritual forces with them. If these are not dealt with they can result in defilement or oppression. I learned this lesson when I first started traveling. I conducted five services in a church that had lost its pastor. The young people were greatly affected. God touched their hearts, snapping them from indifferent irreverence to active participation. By the third service they filled the front rows. Many adults were saved and restored as well.

They invited me back a few months later, but this time the atmosphere was different. I felt surrounded by a heaviness I couldn't shake even while in prayer. I felt as though the weight or burden of the entire church and town were on my shoulders, and I had no anointing or authority to carry it. I even asked God, "Do You want me to stop traveling and pastor this church?" There was no answer. The weight of it was almost unbearable. Finally after almost an hour of struggle I cried out, "Father, what is going on?"

I heard the Holy Spirit's still small voice: "John, the leader and head intercessor are praying that you'll take this church. It is not My will. Break their words, for they are witchcraft." I knew the message was from God for two reasons. First, it brought the first ounce of peace I had since arriving, and second, I had no natural reason to think these two kind people were doing this. God saw beyond what I saw in the natural and told me to break their words. Isaiah says:

> "No weapon formed against you shall prosper, and every tongue which rises against you in judgment you shall condemn. This is the heritage of the servants of the LORD, and their righteousness is from Me," says the LORD.
> —ISAIAH 54:17

Words can be weapons formed against us. These words have spiritual forces behind them. Notice God says we are to condemn those words. I immediately prayed, "Father, according to what You have spoken to me I break every word that has been prayed over my

176

life that is incorrect with Your will. I am not called to come and pastor this church as You have told me; therefore, I render these words powerless against me." Then I went after the demonic powers by saying, "I speak to the forces of darkness that have oppressed me, and I break every manipulating force released against me in the name of my Lord Jesus Christ."

It was as if a well broke open inside of me, and prayer gushed forth when only moments before it had been difficult. The rest of my prayer time was wonderful. I was excited for the service that night.

When service was over I asked the two individuals to meet with me. I shared how God had told me they had been praying I would come and pastor this church. They were surprised but acknowledged they had been praying that way. They shared with great emotion, "No one has ever come to our church before and touched the youth as you have."

I interrupted their statements of validation with, "It is witchcraft!" They looked shocked. I then said, "You are praying your will on my life. God has called me to travel, and you are praying that I would come and take this church!" Both repented, and we proceeded to have wonderful meetings! Hallelujah!

HOW TO HANDLE TRUE PROPHECY

Finally, I need to address what to do with a true prophetic word. The story of Mary the mother of Jesus gives the best illustration. When given the prophetic word from the messenger Gabriel of how she would conceive the Messiah by the Holy Spirit, she simply responded: "Behold the maidservant of the Lord! Let it be to me according to your word" (Luke 1:38).

She did not go and tell all her friends; instead she "kept all these things and pondered them in her heart" (Luke 2:19).

She didn't even tell her fiancé, Joseph. We read:

> Now this is how Jesus the Messiah was born. His mother, Mary, was engaged to be married to Joseph. But while she was still a virgin, she became pregnant by the Holy Spirit. Joseph, her fiancé, being a just man, decided to break the engagement

quietly, so as not to disgrace her publicly.

As he considered this, he fell asleep, and an angel of the Lord appeared to him in a dream. "Joseph, son of David," the angel said, "do not be afraid to go ahead with your marriage to Mary. For the child within her has been conceived by the Holy Spirit."

—MATTHEW 1:18–20, NLT

An angel had to tell Joseph that Mary was not unfaithful to him! Could any of us hold our tongues the way Mary did?

Our culture is not trained to wait and let God work. We are inbred with, "If we don't have it, find a way to get it." So if we don't have the money to buy it, charge it. If sickness strikes, why pray? Call the doctor—we have insurance. If we have been given a promise from God, go for it. Tell everyone. Proclaim it, and through a little manipulation and/or control we can get it. (Of course, we don't say the last part.) Then we claim God fulfilled His promise to us. But in reality we have just birthed another Ishmael.

If God has promised He will do something in your life, let Him.

A wise friend told me years ago, "Make it hard on God. He likes it!" I've never forgotten his words. I've come to realize the harder it is, the more glory He gets! We are only responsible to do what He tells us specifically to do. The rest of the time we believe, pray, fight spiritual opposing forces, and thank God for His fulfillment.

If God tells us to go to a city where He will raise up an international church, our part is to go to the city, pray, and preach. He will make it an international church. If adversity comes against God's word, we handle it through prayer and obedience. But we do not have to help bring forth the prophetic word of promise.

With God's fulfillment it becomes a tree of life for us. As Solomon wrote, "The fruit of the righteous is a tree of life" (Prov. 11:30). And again, "When the desire comes, it is a tree of life" (Prov. 13:12). The one who waits on God and perseveres to His promised fulfillment is an overcomer, and Jesus says, "To him who overcomes I will give to eat from the tree of life" (Rev. 2:7). To wait on Him through prayer, obedience, and thanksgiving is more than worth it!

EPILOGUE

Before concluding, I want to reemphasize two points I made at the beginning of this book. First, the prophetic office is a needed and vital part of the ministry today. Those who do not believe God is still sending prophets are missing a very important element in the ministry of Jesus to His church. Scripture declares that prophets have been given to the church to equip her until we come to the unity of the faith and of the knowledge of the Son of God, to be a perfect man, to the measure of the stature of the fullness of Christ. (See Ephesians 4:11–13.) That has not been accomplished yet, and it won't be until the end of time.

Secondly, we are told not to despise prophecy (1 Thess. 5:20). In fact, Paul tells the church, "Pursue love, and desire spiritual gifts, but especially that you may prophesy" (1 Cor. 14:1). True prophecy is one of the greatest gifts to the body. If we put first things first, which is to pursue the character and glory of God above all things, then our prophesying will be pure.

This message by no means has been written to discourage true prophecy, but has called for us to be vigilant in testing "prophetic utterances," for so much of the "thus saith the Lord's" that are being spoken and written today are not inspired of the Holy Spirit. To judge these utterances is not to despise true prophecy! I want to encourage you to study the third, fourth, and sixth chapters of this book. Examine diligently what God says about New Testament prophets and prophesying. Your understanding of the true will better equip you to recognize the counterfeit.

This book is not complete in itself . . . so much more could be said. Paul warned the believers repeatedly to guard against false ministry that would lead them astray. At one point he pleaded with those at Ephesus day and night for three years. This humble work pales in comparison.

In conclusion I first appeal to those of you in leadership. If I may be so bold in the Lord, leaders, please hear these words: No longer hold back the necessary warnings from those the Holy Spirit has placed under your care. Shepherd the church of God purchased with the precious blood of His Son. The time *has come* when many will no longer heed sound doctrine. Plagued by covetous hearts and itching ears, they will seek out those who will preach a "gospel" that gratifies their self-serving appetites. This will not cease, but will continue to spread, until leadership accepts and walks in the mantle of the Elijah prophetic ministry God is releasing to the church. We must not cling only to the teachings but also to the warnings and corrections of the Lord. Be bold and speak the truth, in the fear of God, and for the love of His people!

To all of us in the church, hear the cry of God through the prophet Jeremiah, these words certainly apply today:

> A horrible and shocking thing has happened in this land—the prophets give false prophecies, and the priests rule with an iron hand (NIV says, "rule by their own authority"). And worse yet, my people like it that way!
> —JEREMIAH 5:30–31, NLT

God calls it *horrible and shocking* when prophets in the church give false prophecies and leaders rule by their own power. Both of these issues have been addressed in earlier chapters. However, what pricks my heart is the next statement. God says, "*Even worse* My people like it!"

I believe the responsibility of the success of the counterfeit rests with each of us in the church who have embraced the counterfeit prophetic. We need to ask ourselves, Why have we given a national platform to ministries that speak to our carnal appetites and desires? Have we desired comfort over truth? Prosperity more than holiness? Anointing and power more than godliness? Have we allowed our desire for the good life to overshadow our desire to see the lost come to Christ? Could these be the reason we have embraced false and flattering words and at times allowed them to bribe us? God warns:

> And you shall take no bribe, for a bribe blinds the discerning and perverts the words of the righteous.
>
> —Exodus 23:8

Has our discernment been blinded by the flattery of false words? Is this why even our own words are perverted? Hear the word of the Lord:

> For no more shall there be any false vision or flattering divination within the house of Israel.
>
> —Ezekiel 12:24

The day is coming when God will clearly separate the flesh from the promise, the counterfeit from the real. Just as with Abraham, the son of promise displaced the son of flesh. In that day, "your watchmen shall lift up their voices, with their voices they shall sing together; for they shall see eye to eye" (Isa. 52:8). The prophetic voices of promise will take their place of service. Until then we must give utmost heed to the following words:

> Now I urge you, brethren, note those who cause divisions and offenses, *contrary to the doctrine which you learned,* and avoid them. For those who are such do not serve our Lord Jesus Christ, but their own belly, and by smooth words and flattering speech deceive the hearts of the simple.
>
> —Romans 16:17–18, emphasis added

To those called to the prophetic ministry who have been

detoured or led astray by what's popular this day, God gives this firm directive:

> If you return, then I will bring you back; you shall stand before Me; if you take out the precious from the vile, you shall be as My mouth. Let them return to you, *but you must not return to them.*
> —JEREMIAH 15:19, EMPHASIS ADDED

A man of God is not what he preaches but what he lives; his message is no greater than what he is. God finds vile our fleshly appetites and desires. When we seek to please ourselves or others more than we seek to please God, we fall prey to the danger of divination, and even worse to become a false prophet. By removing or putting away the evil from before us God promises He will make us His mouthpiece. There is only one sure way of separating this evil, and it is by the fear of the Lord. For:

> . . . by the fear of the LORD one departs from evil.
> —PROVERBS 16:6

When we fear God we will not defer to the desires of man. The fear of the Lord is our greatest need in this day and hour. I believe many will cry out with one heart and voice for its restoration. We are a people of destiny, and we are called by His name to manifest His glory in all the earth! Hallelujah!

I leave you with these words the Lord dropped in my heart only this morning as I completed this work.

> One thing I have desired of the LORD, that will I seek: that I may dwell in the house of the LORD all the days of my life, to behold the beauty of the LORD, and to inquire in His temple.
> —PSALM 27:4

May this always be our deepest and strongest desire.

NOTES

FOREWORD

1. Ted Haggard, "Handling False Prophecy," *Ministries Today,* September/October 1998, p. 29.

CHAPTER 2: WIDESPREAD DECEPTION

1. Ibid.

CHAPTER 7: SPEAKING TO THE IDOLS OF THE HEART

1. *Vine's Complete Expository Dictionary of Biblical Words* (Nashville, TN: Thomas Nelson, 1985), s.v. "to save."
2. Ibid., s.v. "iniquity."

CHAPTER 10: THE OPERATION OF JEZEBEL

1. *The Online Bible Thayer's Greek Lexicon,* copyright © 1993, Woodside Bible Fellowship, Ontario, Canada. Licensed from the Institute for Creation Research.

CHAPTER 11: SELF OR GOD APPOINTED

1. *The Interlinear Bible,* volume II, p. 750.

CHAPTER 13: KNOWING PROPHETS BY THEIR FRUIT

1. W. E. Vine, *Vine's Expository Dictionary of Biblical Words* (Nashville, TN: Thomas Nelson Publishers, 1985), s.v. "heresy."

Other Books by
John and Lisa Bevere

THE FEAR OF THE LORD by John Bevere

 More than ever, there's something missing in our churches, our prayers, and in our personal lives. It's what builds intimacy in our relationship with God. It's what makes our lives real and pure. It's what transforms us into truly Spirit-led children of God. It is the fear of the Lord.

This book exposes our need to fear God and challenges us to reverence God anew in our worship and daily lives. This profound message will provoke you to honor God in a way that will revolutionize your life.

THE BAIT OF SATAN by John Bevere
Your Response Determines Your Future

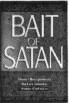 This book exposes one of the most deceptive snares Satan uses to get believers out of the will of God. It is the trap of offense.

Most who are ensnared do not even realize it. But everyone must be made aware of this trap, because Jesus said, "It is impossible that offenses will not come" (Luke 17:1). The question is not, "Will you encounter the bait of Satan?" Rather it is, "How will you respond?" *Your response determines your future!* Don't let another person's sin or mistake affect your relationship with God!

> "This book by my friend John Bevere is strong, strong, strong! I found new help from his fresh insights and uncompromising desire to help each of us recognize Satan's baits and avoid them at all costs."
> —*Oral Roberts, Oral Roberts University*

BREAKING INTIMIDATION   by John Bevere
How to Overcome Fear and Release the Gift of God in Your Life

Countless Christians battle intimidation. Yet they wrestle with the side effects rather than the source. Intimidation is rooted in the fear of man. Proverbs 29:25 says, "The fear of man brings a snare . . ." This snare limits us so we don't reach our full potential.

Paul admonished Timothy, "The gift of God in you is dormant because you're intimidated!" (2 Tim. 1:6–7, paraphrased). An intimidated believer loses his position of spiritual authority. Without this authority his gifting from God remains dormant.

The Bible is filled with examples of God's people facing intimidation. Some overcame while others were overcome. This book is an in-depth look at these ancient references and present-day scenarios. The goal: to expose intimidation, break its fearful grip, and release God's gift and dominion in your life.

This is an urgent message for every child of God who desires to reach their full potential in their walk with Christ. Don't allow fear to hold you back!

THE DEVIL'S DOOR   by John Bevere

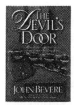

In *The Bait of Satan,* John Bevere exposed the devil's number-one trap for believers today. In *The Devil's Door,* he reveals the easiest way the enemy gains access in the lives of Christians—through rebellion. Satan cleverly deceives believers into thinking that submission is bondage and that rebellion is freedom. This revealing book exposes the devil's deception, blocks his entrance into your life, and helps you enjoy God's blessing and protection.

■ This book contains challenging and life-changing truths.
■ What is the source of true kingdom authority?
■ Learn to shut this door and lock it!

VICTORY IN THE WILDERNESS *by John Bevere*
God, Where Are You?

Is this the cry of your heart? Does it seem your spiritual progress in the Lord has come to a halt—or even regressed? You wonder if you have missed God or somehow displeased Him, but that is not the case . . . you've just arrived at the wilderness! Now, don't misunderstand the purpose of the wilderness. It is not God's rejection, but the season of His preparation in your life. God intends for you to have *Victory in the Wilderness.*

Understanding this season is crucial to the successful completion of your journey. It is the road traveled by patriarchs and prophets in preparation for a fresh move of God.

Some issues addressed in this book:

- How God refines
- Pressing through dry times
- Why *where you are* is vital to *where you're going*
- Is the wilderness necessary?
- What is the focus of the true prophetic?

THE VOICE OF ONE CRYING *by John Bevere*
A Prophetic Message for Today!

God is restoring the prophetic to turn the hearts of His people to Him. Yet often this office is reduced to merely one who predicts the future by a word of knowledge or wisdom . . . rather than a declaration of the church's true condition and destiny. Many, fed up with hype and superficial ministry, are ready to receive the true prophetic message.

Some issues addressed in this book:

- Genuine vs. counterfeit conversion
- Recognizing false prophets
- Idolatry in America
- Message of the true prophetic
- The Elijah anointing
- Exposing deception

YOU ARE NOT WHAT YOU WEIGH by Lisa Bevere

Are you tired of reading trendy diet books, taking faddish pills, and ordering the latest in television infomercial exercise equipment? If you're like most women, what you're really tired of is the tyranny of dieting.

Break free from the destructive cycle of dieting and apprehend true freedom. Discover riveting truths from God's Word with the power to set you free. Trade your *self* consciousness for a deeper consciousness of God.

OUT OF CONTROL AND LOVING IT! by Lisa Bevere

Is your life a whirlwind of turmoil? Are you hating it? It is because you are in control! In this candid and honest book, Lisa challenges you to relinquish control of your life to God. Are you tired of pretending to be free only to remain captive? This book contains in-depth insight into how fear causes us to hold on when we should let go! Are you holding on? Abandon yourself to God's care!

- Escaping captivity
- Overcoming anger
- Your past is not your future

- Conquering fear
- The strongholds of gossip
- Self neglect vs. self denial

THE TRUE MEASURE OF A WOMAN by Lisa Bevere

A woman often measures herself and her own worth according to the standards set by others around her. Her self-esteem rises and falls with the whims of popular opinion as she allows other people to control how she thinks about herself.

In her frank, yet gentle manner, Lisa exposes the subtle influences and blatant lies that hold many women captive. This is an interactive book designed with questions to help you unveil the truth of God's Word. These truths will displace any lies and also help you discover who you are in Christ. It is only then that you can stop comparing yourself to others and begin to see yourself as God loves you.

Audio/Visual Messages:

By John and Lisa Bevere

Videos
The Bait of Satan
The Baptism of Fire
Breaking Intimidation
Does God Know You?
Don't Faint Before Your Harvest
The Fear of the Lord
Passion for His Presence
Cultivating a Pure Heart
Secret to God's Outpouring
Changed From Glory to Glory

Audiocassette Series (3 tapes)
Armed to Suffer
By Order of the King
The Fear of the Lord
Pursue the High Call
Standing Strong in a World of Compromise
The Training Ground of Champions
Walking With God
Out of Control and Loving It! (Lisa Bevere)

To order call 1-800-648-1477 (U.S. only)
or 407-889-9617

PLEASE CONTACT JOHN BEVERE MINISTRIES:
■ To receive JBM's free newsletter, *The Messenger*
■ To receive a **FREE** and COMPLETE COLOR CATALOg
■ To inquire about inviting the ministry of
John and Lisa Bevere to your organization

JOHN BEVERE MINISTRIES
P. O. Box 2002
Apopka, FL 32704-2002
Tel: 407-889-9617
Fax: 407-889-2065
E-mail: jbm@johnbevere.org
Website: www.johnbevere.org

In Europe, please contact the ministry at:

JOHN BEVERE MINISTRIES INTERNATIONAL LTD.
P.O. Box 138
Lichfield
WE14 OYL
United Kingdom
Tel./Fax: 44-1543-483383
E-mail:jbeurope@johnbevere.org

The Messenger television program aires on The Christian
Channel Europe. Please check your local listings for day and time.

You can experience more of *God's grace & love!*